MW00938724

College Recruiting Hacked:

Your Path To Becoming A College Athlete

Fred Bastie

ISBN 9781523285730

Every effort has been made to provide accurate links at the time of publication; however, the author assumes no responsibility for changes which occur after publication to the links or content. The author does not have any control over and does not assume any responsibility for websites or their content.

Dedication

This book is dedicated to the 98%. The 98% of student-athletes with the desire and ability to play in college, but who are not highly recruited. College recruiting does not have to be the frustrating, complicated, expensive process many people make it out to be. This book is a guide for the 98%, to level the playing field and allow them to pursue their dream.

Thank you

A special thanks to all the people who contributed to, inspired and made this book and Playced.com possible. First and foremost, thanks to my wife, Sheri for her help, support and understanding as we set out to change an industry. Thanks to my children, Reed and Brooke for inspiring this book and always being available for their dad.

A very special thanks to our team of Playced executives and experts including our President Ross Hawley, Executive Vice-President Pat Leach and Social Media Director Pat Hade. They have kept me on track, edited my rambling content and focused my thoughts.

Thanks to our investors who believe in the Playced mission and have made it possible for us to help student-athletes across the country. This book would not have been possible without their trust and support.

Finally, thanks to those supporters who have helped develop the concept of Playced.com and the content for this book including Kim Trant, Katherine Konstans and Gil Brandt.

Fred Bastie

Table of Contents

The Preseason 1

The Mental Work Begins 4

Myth 1 4

Myth 2 8

Myth 3 10

Myth 4 12

Myth 5 13

Myth 6 15

Myth 7 17

Myth 8 19

Myth 9 21

Myth 10 24

Be Careful with Recruiting Companies 26

Know Where You Fit 30

Know the School 30

Know the Finances 31

Know What Hurts You 32

Know What You Have To Do 33

Develop a Recruiting Game Plan 35

How Parents/Guardians Can Help 41

The College Coach's Perspective 51

8 Common Mistakes Made By Recruits 55

Setting Goals 61

Commit to being realistic 69

Commit to the process 71

Commit to being persistent 71

Freshman Year 73

Set Your Goals 74

Get the Grades 74

Know the Amateur Rules 75

Learn to Use Social Media..76

Plan High School Courses 77

Research Colleges and Universities and Develop a Favorites List..78

Research Showcases and Camps..............................80

Develop a plan for Elite/Club Teams 84

Start an Athletic Resume & Video Archive 87

Freshman Home-Schooled Athletes 89

Sophomore Year 90

Register...91

Sorry about this one - Take the PSAT 91

Learn How Your Sport Evaluates Athletes..............92

Set Up A Meeting With Your Coaches 94

How Your Coach Can Help..96

Discuss the Family College Budget...........................97

Update Your Favorite Colleges List 98

Check that you are on track with your courses......99

Review your Skills Development and Plan 99

Continue Building Your Athletic Resume...............99

Send Initial Contact Emails to Coaches on Your
Favorites List..100

Junior Year 102

Updates 103

Prepare for and take the SAT or ACT 103

Create a Highlight Video 105

Clean up your Social Media...................................107

Review your progress with your Guidance
Counselor...108

Ask your coach to assess your abilities.................109

Get your coach involved as a reference................109

Review and update your list of colleges 110

Go on Unofficial Visits..110

Prepare questions to ask college coaches during
your unofficial visit...111

Prepare for questions a coach might ask..............113

Attend Camps/Combines/Showcases that make
sense 116

Follow Up Emails 117

Keep in contact with coaches 118

Financial Aid Forms 118

Don't compare..119

SAT/ACT Scores 120

Don't get discouraged 120

Senior Year 121

Go on Official visits.................................122

Take serious Senior courses 122

Retake the SAT/ACT if you think that you can get a higher score 123

Dial down on reaching out to colleges 123

Review and update your Favorite Colleges List....124

Meet with your coach to review his or her assessment of your abilities................................124

Keep in contact with College Coaches 125

Finalize Finances.................................125

After You Sign..................................126

Post Season...................129

Why it's Worth It..129

Future Employers 129

Relationships 134

Appendix 1: Recruiting Rules and Definitions.................................136

NCAA, NAIA and NJCAA 136

NCAA Vocabulary 142

Academic Rules..149

Appendix 2: The Difference Between Being Noticed and Being Recruited 153

You are not being recruited if: 153

You've been noticed, but you are not being recruited 154

You are being recruited 155

Appendix 3: Scholarships, Teams, Athletes 157

Appendix 4: Recruiting Videos 162

Meet the Author 171

Illustrations Credits...............................173

The Preseason

You've decided you really want to become a college athlete; actually you can't imagine not continuing your career at the next level. Announce that and suddenly everyone has opinions, advice, and long-winded suggestions on how to "get recruited." People bombard you with their own recruiting stories. Friends talk about the amount of money they paid recruiters to get their information in front of the right coaches. Players, coaches, and friends of friends of friends all have something to add. Turn online for help and there are hundreds of thousands of articles, eBooks and promotions. Suddenly, playing in college looks more complex and harder than Inorganic Chemistry.

Becoming a college athlete is not the vastly complex, totally confusing, incredibly intimidating, exorbitantly expensive process a lot of people would have you believe it is. This book is a roadmap to playing in college. The steps are simple. You can follow each step. We set out the work and timelines for that work. You're an athlete, you know how to be disciplined at working towards a goal. The process is the process. You can, and should, control that process!
 At the root of the college recruiting process there is one undeniable fact; no one has more of an investment in your future than you do. Not

your coaches, teachers, recruiters, or even your guardians and parents. Your goals. Your life. Your future.

Ready to start?

Recruiting Reality

College recruiting isn't rocket science. A lot of it is common sense. So let's start with the reality of playing at the next level.

Statistically, only about 2% of high school athletes will play in college. However, and it's a huge however, that still means that every year 460,000 young men and women play NCAA college sports and 65,000 more play at the 250+ NAIA colleges. If you work at your skills and work hard in the classroom, there's no reason that you can't be in that half-a-million player pool. It does mean that there is mental, physical, and emotional work involved in getting there. It does mean that you have to have a good process to get to where you want to be.

If you already know the recruiting terminology, the NAIA, DIII, Quiet Period type of terms, then read on. If not take a detour to the Appendix Section so the rest of this makes sense.

The Mental Work Begins

The first step in a realistic recruiting journey is to get rid of the myths that surround recruiting and that you've probably heard delivered as "facts" for your entire playing career.

Myth 1

If you are good enough, college coaches will find you.

Fact: Just because you are a good athlete, you can't settle back, enjoy your high school years and be pretty much assured of a free ride to college. Recruiting just doesn't work that way for most athletes.

College coaches have recruiting budgets, and with the exception of Division I Football and Basketball, those budgets are limited. They can't afford to travel the country looking for recruits. Therefore, if you wait around to get recruited, it may never happen, even if you are "good enough." As a junior or senior in high school if you are currently being "under-recruited," you need to reach out to the colleges on your own. If you don't, the chances of a college coach finding you is about as likely as finding the proverbial needle in a haystack.

When you are a standout athlete at the national level, college coaches will put you on their "look at" list. But, before you get to their "recruit them" list, there are a number of hurdles. These hurdles are faced by all recruits of every level as they move from the "look at" to the "talk to" lists.

#1 Academics

You must qualify academically. Coaches will not bother with you if you are academically ineligible, period. A few well-funded schools might be willing to take a chance and red-shirt a player who is one of the best in the nation, but most are opposed to gambling on an athlete in the hope that they get the grades during that first college year to change their eligibility. So let's get that settled immediately; grades really matter.

For those of you who want to potentially play at the NCAA DI level, you must have the minimum

2.3 GPA in NCAA Core Courses and a minimum 900 on your Verbal and Math SAT, or a combined 75 on your ACT.   (see the section on Rules and Regulations.) For NCAA DII, a 2.2 in NCAA core courses will be required starting August 1, 2018 and there is also a sliding scale of combined test scores and core-course grade-point averages. Currently, the DII GPA requirement is 2.0. NCAA DIII schools have their own academic requirements which are often much tougher than DI and DII. NAIA schools require that you meet 2 of these criteria: 2.0 or better GPA; top 50% of your graduating class; ACT score of 18 or SAT combined score of 860.

#2   Fit into the Program

You really need to fit in with a program's culture. College coaches look to social media and recommendations from your current coaches to get a sense of a player. Many promising recruits have been dropped because of their social media feeds.   A high school coach's opinion can drastically change how an athlete is recruited, as well. Not making the list doesn't necessarily mean you're not a good student/athlete/person. It just means that most college coaches are very sensitive to the makeup of their team and won't sacrifice team chemistry for one recruit.

#3 Fill a Need

The colleges have to anticipate a need for your skill set or position during your college years. You have absolutely no control over their roster, but if you're a point guard and there are 4 point guards already on the roster it is going to be harder to be recruited by that college. On the other hand, if you're a center and the college's roster doesn't have a presence in the post, the program is going to have more interest in you.

Review the team roster for the colleges you decide to pursue to be sure you are being realistic. If you are a high school freshman starting the recruiting process, you should watch which players colleges recruit each year and adjust your list accordingly.

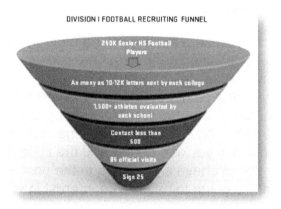

DIVISION I FOOTBALL RECRUITING FUNNEL

250K Senior HS Football Players

As many as 10-12K letters sent by each college

1,500+ athletes evaluated by each school

Contact less than 500

85 official visits

Sign 25

Myth 2

Many student-athletes feel that if they have been invited to a college camp, receive an email from a coach, or are sent a questionnaire they are being recruited and can ease up on pursuing other options.

Fact: When you get a camp invite it may simply mean that there is some very preliminary interest in you - which is a huge leap from "being recruited." Or, it can just mean that you're in the geographic area the camp draws from. College Camps are times for coaches to take a more in-depth look at players; they are also a method of adding income to the financial picture of the program. An invitation to a camp lets you get a chance to know the coaches a bit and to show your work-ethic. But you are part of a large group so don't pin your hopes on one school who invited you to a camp.

And, while a questionnaire shows some initial interest, the numbers are pretty staggering.

A DI football program may send out as many as 10,000-12,000 letters for 25 open positions; that's an average of 440 letters for every athlete who will eventually play for the program. Only about 1 in 20 athletes who get a personal phone call from a college coach will ever play for that coach. That doesn't mean you should dismiss the questionnaire; fill it out. It does mean that you shouldn't assume that there is special interest in you and stop your other recruiting efforts.

The bottom line is that until you are absolutely certain that you are going to play for a program you need to keep your recruiting efforts going.

Myth 3

My coach, parents or someone else will find my scholarship.

Fact: Don't believe that other people are going to do your recruiting for you. Most athletes feel that it is their high school coach's job to find their scholarship, and some believe that putting a video on a recruiting site will yield a mailbox full of offers. None of those beliefs mirror reality.

Your current coaches shouldn't do the work for you. Their job is to help you play your sport as well as you can, to build a team that is proud of their effort and to teach the sport. Most High School coaches are willing to write recommendations or talk to college coaches, but don't ask them to find you a college scholarship; that is not their job.

There are also recruiting sites that imply that an online profile will guarantee that college coaches are looking at your information. Recruiting Sites may be a way for coaches who are already interested in you to check you out, but they are not outreach sites. The average College Coach works 90+ hours a week. Do you really think they're spending the majority of their free time looking through recruiting sites? Recruiting sites are not discovery sites.

NCAA DIII NAIA
NCAA DI NCAA DII
NJCAA

Myth 4

Division I is the only/best option.

Fact: Because Division I athletics are heavily covered by the media there is a belief that DI is the best option, or the only option if an athlete wants a scholarship or to play highly competitive college athletics. Not true.

If you want to pursue your sport professionally, you want to make it your career, then DI is considered the best option. If you need some time to develop while you continue to play, or if your career will not be in your sport, there are many other options. You can find a partial athletic scholarship in most sports at the NCAA Division II, NAIA and junior college levels. NCAA DIII schools don't give athletic scholarships but provide financial aid to student-athletes in other forms. Many of these programs are highly competitive.

Myth 5

Recruiting starts your Junior Year of High School

Fact: For most athletes the recruiting process should start freshman year, although many student-athletes erroneously believe that their recruiting efforts should start their junior year in high school. The reason for that may be that September 1 of your junior year is the first time coaches of many sports can reach out to you unless you have signed a NLI (National Letter of Intent) with the program. That doesn't mean that coaches aren't aware of players and watching players well before their Junior Year. They can also respond to athletes who have contacted them prior to that date. College coaches can put you on their potential lists prior to that date, invite you to camps and watch you play. NCAA DIII can talk to athletes at any time, as can NAIA Coaches. The NCAA used to tell student-athletes to register their Junior year; they now suggest that you register with their NCAA Eligibility Center at the beginning of your sophomore year.

Recruiting really is a long term process; you need a 4 year recruiting game plan.

Myth 6

Athletes and their parents think they need to have a professionally made recruiting video.

Fact: While a professional video set to inspirational music might make your grandparents happy, it's just not necessary. With the apps and hubs and the quality of videos you can take from mobile phones today, you can certainly display your skills on video without spending a fortune. YouTube has an excellent and easy-to-use video editing feature which also allows you to add annotations, music (if you must) and embed links in the video. Facebook's video editing capability is getting fairly sophisticated. The idea of a recruiting video is to show what you can bring to the college program; not how artistic you are.

As a side-myth, video isn't just for football players. Each sport is looking for different information on the video, but all college coaches appreciate being able to see the potential recruits' capabilities. (See the section on Recruiting Videos for more information.)

Myth 7

Many student-athletes and their parents/guardians believe that college coaches don't want to be contacted by prospective athletes.

Fact: If you don't ask the answer is always "No." Athletes hesitate to contact college coaches fearing that they will look desperate, or be a pest, or annoy the coach. In reality if you are a good fit for the program athletically and a good fit academically then you are helping the coach out and they'll be glad to hear from you.

There are ways to contact a coach for the first time and they do not include sending a DM that says "Wassup? Check out my video" with a link. You're trying to earn a roster spot not join a local gang. Think of your first contact as the equivalent of meeting a coach at a camp for the first time. Polite, succinct and respectful go a long way to creating a good first impressions and those contacts are welcomed by coaches.

Myth 8

Athletes have been conditioned to believe they need to use a professional recruiter or recruiting company to find a roster spot and/or to land a scholarship.

Fact: Professional recruiters may have given you an advantage in the pre-tech world because they had access to databases and contact information that the athlete didn't. But today student-athletes have access to that same information.

Professional Recruiters come with a pretty hefty price tag ranging from just under a thousand dollars for a limited package to several thousand dollars. Add to that the fact that recruiting is an unregulated, uncertified industry, so the only thing that's required to be a "Recruiter" is to declare you are a "Recruiter." Actually you could decide tomorrow that you want to be a recruiter and go into business. If you do talk to compensated recruiters, be certain that they are working with a reputable company that knows the business and that they will tell you their price ranges before they know your zip code.

With the technology available to student-athletes today, much of what one used to pay a recruiter for can be done by the student-athlete. And it is your journey. College coaches have specifically told me they want to hear from the athlete; they want to see the athlete personally show initiative. In a survey of college coaches many said that they treat email or calls from compensated recruiters as spam. Reputable recruiting firms will tell you up-front that they can guide you, but you have to do the work yourself. So if the technology is available, you have to do the work yourself anyhow and college coaches prefer to hear from you, it doesn't make any sense to pay someone else to talk you through the process.

Myth 9

The recruiting process has to be really expensive.

Fact: If you listen to enough horror stories about recruiting you'll actually believe this myth. The recruiting process doesn't have to be expensive. Let's repeat that, it doesn't have to be beyond your financial reach. College recruiting does not have to drain the college fund.

Be smart with your recruiting dollars by being selective in lessons, camps, and select/club teams. They can all be very important in developing a college athlete, but all three can also be expensive. No amount of money poured into your college preparation will definitely ensure a college scholarship or even a spot on a college roster. Specialized lessons that make you a better player are probably a good investment although a good school coaching staff can usually teach you a lot. With few exceptions, college coaches attend showcases, camps and clinics as a means to evaluate players they have already identified, not to find new prospects. So don't think that if you spend a bunch of money on a camp you will be noticed. And don't think that if you don't go to a camp or can't take lessons from a former Olympian that you won't be recruited.

The bottom line is that nothing pays bigger dividends than consistent hard work. Your High School coach's recommendation will count heavily in the recruiting process and you control your relationship with your coach.

For select/club teams, you don't have to be on the best team. You just need to be on a team that plays quality competition and has good coaching.

When it comes to other costs such as videos, trips to tournaments/camps unofficial visits to schools, and using a compensated recruiter, each family should budget an amount that makes sense for them and is in line with the goals of the athlete. Many, many athletes have no intention of ever playing professionally and their college recruiting is going to be a different experience then an athlete for whom college athletics is a step on a sports career path; keep that in mind when you're deciding how to spend money on recruiting.

Myth 10

Many people believe that a scholarship will take care of all the financial needs for college.

Fact: That's definitely not the case. Most athletic scholarships are not "full rides;" full rides are offered at the Division I level in the "head count" sports. These include FBS Football, Men's and Women's Basketball, Women's Tennis, Women's Gymnastics and Women's Volleyball. All other Division I sports are equivalency sports and partial scholarships are the norm ranging from 25% to 60% of tuition. Division II, NAIA and Junior colleges also offer equivalency scholarships. NCAA Division III schools don't offer athletic scholarships but use academic scholarships, grants and other forms of financial aid to help their student-athletes.

Since the average college budget for an in-state public college is over $20,000 and a moderate budget for a private school is over $40,000, if you are seeking a scholarship in an equivalency sport, you still have some financial planning to do. Academic awards, need-based grants, and other financial aid should be part of your research.

Now that we've dispelled the myths, we're going to look at one more pitfall in the recruiting process that can waste time and money; recruiting services.

Be Careful with Recruiting Companies

If you search the internet for recruiting help, you will find that there are almost as many recruiting services/websites as there are colleges. Many promise they will help you find an athletic scholarship because they have access to people and information you don't, or they imply that college coaches spend hours each day looking through their athlete profiles, or that the process is so difficult that you need a personal guide.

As in any industry, there are good recruiting services and there are companies that are just trying to separate you from your dollars. Here are the things you should consider if you are thinking about hiring a recruiting company.

1. Recruiting services aren't miracle workers. They can't make you run faster, jump higher or throw harder. They also can't change three years of poor grades in high school. You have to be realistic about your academic and athletic abilities or your college recruiting experience will be disappointing no matter how much you spend on recruiting assistance.

2. You have to be involved in the process even if you use a $2500.00+ service. You don't write a check to a recruiting service

and wait for your National Letter of Intent to arrive in the mail. You will have to send out emails, talk to the coaching staff at the colleges, go through progress with the recruiter and do the work.

Credible recruiting services educate the athlete and the parent on how the recruiting process works. Keep that in mind when you are making a decision about a recruiting company.

Questions to ask when deciding whether or not to use a recruiting service

How much does your service cost? You need to understand the "all in" cost of their "premium" package. If the recruiter isn't willing to answer this question, or if they have to interview you before giving you a price range, run for the hills!

How involved will I be in the process? The more involved you are in the process, the better the result, but if you are going to do all the work then the service should be relatively inexpensive.

Will you provide my personal information to other companies? Unless you want to be inundated with emails, promotional giveaways and phone calls then you should ask this question. Some services have relationships with other companies and your personal information will be passed along.

How will you identify the colleges to contact? This question is critical. Make sure the answer makes sense. Are they just going to send out emails to every program in the country? Do they just put you in a PDF that gets sent to coaches once a month? Are they just sending emails to the colleges they have relationships with? Exactly what criteria are being used to craft your future?

Will you contact colleges on my behalf and if so, how many? If you aren't currently a four-star recruit, then to some extent the recruiting process is a numbers game. If they are contacting schools on your behalf, make sure you know how many, which ones and what that contact consists of. There is no reason to contact colleges in which you have no interest. It's also not helpful if you are one of 300 athletes' information in a newsletter that they are sending to coaches.

What criteria will you use to determine the colleges to pursue? Make sure they will be considering the things that are important to you. Remember, you have to live there for four years!

At the risk of being redundant, this is your recruiting journey. If you decide to use a service, do your homework, read the reviews, ask the right questions and understand exactly what you are paying for. If you decide to do it yourself, educate yourself on the process and be persistent.

Other Services

In the last few years several additional services have started which purport to help recruits be noticed using social media. We're not talking about services that help you clean up your social media but those that will "promote" you via their own social media, for a fee. In all honestly, unless those services are tagging specific coaches your chance of getting seen by a coach whose college fits your academic/athletic abilities are worse than your chances of winning Power Ball. And, again, you can tag college coaches in your social media yourself.

Free Website profiles

There are some platforms that do have free website profiles, Hudl being one of them. There are others who will only show your information after you have been "verified" by their staff in an interview. Check the fine print before you take your time to fill out a "free profile" on a recruiting site. You also want to know if the site keeps your non-public information private or whether they share that information with other companies.

Recruiting Stories

Know Where You Fit
One recent recruit had a 34 on his ACT test, a 4.64 time in the 40, and was an All-District wide receiver in high school. Sounds like a possible Division I prospect, right? Well, that is what he and his parents thought, but initially they had their eyes only on elite Division I programs like LSU and Alabama. They didn't understand why their emails to the recruiting coordinators for Coach Miles and Coach Saban resulted in very little interest. They posted a highlight video on a recruiting site, but the "coach views" weren't from schools they were interested in. The family and the athlete had some harrowing months. They just didn't realize how narrow the funnel gets for elite Division I programs.

Once this family started to contact more appropriate colleges, the recruiting process actually became exciting. Ultimately, this athlete signed at an Ivy League school and based on his ACT score that probably would have been a good starting point.

Know the School
The first camp this recruit attended was at a Division I school in North Carolina. In his first at bat, he hit the fence. He pitched extremely well, and by the end of the camp, all the coaches knew his name. His dad was ready to pack the

U-Haul for North Carolina until, on the last day of the camp they went on a tour of the campus with some former baseball players. Since his son wanted to study engineering, the father asked where the engineering school was located. The answer? "We don't have one of those." Let's see… airfare to Charlotte, rental car, hotel room for three days, restaurants, camp fee…you get the picture. They wasted a lot of time and money because they didn't do their homework. They just assumed every major college has an engineering department.

Know the Finances

A few years ago, one of the best catchers in Texas was going through the recruiting process. His heart's desire was to play baseball at a particular private school. Since he was one of the top prospects in the state, several Division I colleges recruited him, including the college he preferred. Although this school actually offered him a good scholarship, the tuition and fees there were not affordable even with the partial scholarship. He eventually signed at a junior college at the last minute and later transferred to an in-state public school where the tuition and fees with a partial scholarship were within his family's budget. Realistically, he shouldn't have been looking at the private school at all; he should have focused on in-state public schools that were affordable, or he should have explored the possibility of other financial aid.

Know What Hurts You

This 6'8" shooting guard was finishing his junior high school season and was being pursued by at least 15 Division I basketball programs. He had it all; very good grades, a 31 on his ACT, had played on the best summer team and he was MVP of his district. It seemed as though he would have his choice of colleges, but one Friday night after a game he made a poor decision. He posted an inappropriate tweet about a female classmate. Shortly after he hit "enter" he deleted the post, but it was there long enough for it to be seen by the girl, a few teammates and some players from opposing teams.

The next week, he was suspended from his team for one game and communication from college coaches slowed down significantly. Luckily, he reached out for advice on how to handle the situation. He listened to the advice and handled the situation the right way. He apologized to the classmate, to his team and to the school administration. A few college coaches asked about the incident and when they did, he answered their questions by explaining that he made a mistake. His heartfelt apology along with a promise that a lesson had been learned was received well by the college coaches. He later signed with a Division I basketball program at the college he was most interested in. Be mindful that lots of inappropriate posts cannot be fixed with an apology. He got lucky; a lot of recruits have sabotaged themselves with social media.

Know What You Have To Do

Playing football in a small town can make recruiting a challenge. Add to that having to play nose guard at 190 pounds when you will most likely be a linebacker or safety in college made being proactive essential for this football recruit. As a junior, this athlete had received NO interest from college coaches and he was devastated because football was his passion. He realized that the NFL was not in his future, so being realistic wasn't an issue. The problem was getting noticed by college coaches.

In the summer between his junior and senior year, his parents challenged him to take ownership of his recruiting process. He signed up with Playced.com and committed a few hours a month to reaching out to at least 20 college coaches at schools that made sense for his ability level. He asked his coach to be involved and he followed up with each and every college. He set up a Twitter account specifically for his football recruiting efforts. In the fall of his senior year, he was being recruited by 8 Division II colleges and had interest from a few Division I colleges. Eventually, he signed with a large Division II college, close to home and one that offered the major he was most interested in. This is how college recruiting really works.

In all of these recruits' journeys there were some rough months that could have been avoided. The University of Arizona's Coach Mike Candrea, one of the nation's most respected softball coaches, had some great advice for recruits:

"Recruiting is the process of gaining knowledge and knowledge is power. Do your homework on these schools, the same way they do their homework on you."

Let's get to the Recruiting Gameplan so we make sure you minimize your problems and maximize your potential.

Develop a Recruiting Game Plan

Less than 2% of high school athletes are highly recruited by college coaches. By my calculations, that leaves 98% of high school athletes to fend for themselves.

The world of college recruiting grows more and more competitive, each year. With athletes verbally committing to colleges as early as 8th grade, it's safe to say recruiting isn't what it used to be. Rising scholarship values, combined with higher coaching salaries, have turned student-athletes into an institutional investment, to say the least.

If you are a 6'4" left-handed pitcher with a 94 MPH fastball or a 5'11" female point guard with 13 assists a game, the colleges will find you. But what if you are a 5'10", 135 lb., right-handed pitcher with an 88 MPH fastball who has the ability and desire to play in college, but just aren't getting noticed by the kind of colleges you want to attend? Like anything in life, you need to have a workable game plan to maximize your chances of landing the right scholarship. Treat the recruiting process like a long, drawn out job interview.

So, what does a good recruiting game plan look like? At its core, it's a 3 step process.

Step 1: Get Real

"Reaching out to schools that are not appropriate is really a waste of their time and our time. Identifying the right colleges is perhaps the hardest part of recruiting for any athlete."
Coach Thompson, Head Men's Basketball Coach
The University of Texas at San Antonio

Setting realistic expectations is critical to any successful recruiting game plan. This is by far the hardest and most important part of the process for every recruit. If you cannot be realistic with who you are as a student and who you are as an athlete, you will struggle with the recruiting process. Not every high school football player can make the roster at Alabama. Not every female basketball player can make the cut at Baylor. Pursuing colleges that aren't an athletic and academic match is a recipe for disaster.

Pursue colleges that should have as much interest in you as you have in them. You have a limited time to find the right fit; don't waste it on schools that are out of reach. If you are unsure about where you fit athletically, ask your current coach for an honest evaluation of what level colleges are appropriate, but be prepared for an honest answer. If you are unsure about which colleges would be a match for your academic qualifications, ask your high school guidance counselor for help, do your own research, or use a website designed to connect you with appropriate colleges.

It is also important to pick a college where you will be happy if you end up not playing. Make sure your choices fit your preferences (size, location, major, budget, etc.). Not all schools offer a degree in marine biology, veterinary medicine or elementary particle physics, for example, and not all college athletic scholarships are full rides.

Pursuing schools that aren't a match for you is going to make the recruiting process difficult and might result in a miserable college experience.

Step 2: Get Connected

"Student-athletes and their families should know that college coaches really appreciate hearing

from a recruit that has specific interest in their program."
Theresa Romagnolo, Head Women's Soccer Coach Notre Dame University

Zig Ziglar once said, "If you aim at nothing, you will hit it every time." The same rule holds true for communicating with college coaches. How is a college supposed to be interested in you if they don't know you exist? There are over 1,000,000 high school football players in the United States, a college coach can't go through 1,000,000 profiles to find you. And, the only way they know you have an interest in their program is for you to tell them you have an interest in their program. As Coach Russ Rose, the legendary Penn State Volleyball said:

"One of the major reasons we have had success at Penn State is because the majority of our recruits sell us on why we should take them, not the opposite. Success is about knowing what you want and making it happen, the same can be said about college recruiting."

Unless you have numerous college coaches continually reaching out to you, you have to contact colleges on your own. Contacting college coaches is the second piece of the puzzle for a successful recruiting game plan and requires an organized, well thought out communication strategy. This is where you set the stage for a successful recruiting experience.

You want to distinguish yourself from the other recruits, especially the ones who play your position and have similar athletic abilities.

Connecting with the coach on a personal level will pay big dividends. For example, if the school just won a conference championship you should congratulate the coach. If you have a relative who attended the school, or if you are interested in a specific major they offer, mention it. In fact, last year the recruiting coordinator at a Big 12 college told me; "If a high school athlete takes the time to write me a personal email or letter, I feel obliged to respond."

Remember, your first email is just to generate interest; this is a process. You have to be persistent and don't expect to receive a response to every email. Don't take that personally. College coaches are busy; however, when you do receive a personal response, you need to respond promptly.

For the colleges that don't respond, send a follow-up email in a few weeks reiterating your interest.

Step 3: Get Organized

If you are using a service like Playced.com the technology will pretty much force you to be organized. If you are not, then keep track of progress on a spreadsheet. Keep all the contact information of the college coaches in columns. Note which colleges you have contacted and where you stand in the process. As you visit college websites, gather information, and research those programs that interest you; add the important information. That research will let you personalize your introductory email or letter and help you determine which schools work best for you.

The Role of Adults in Your Recruiting Gameplan

"Support your kids, give them honest feedback and help them to develop educated opinions. A supportive parent means so much in the positive development of a student-athlete." Coach Rose, Penn State

In a perfect world, your parent(s)/guardian(s) have taken on a supportive role in your athletic endeavors. Hopefully they don't believe that your success in athletics is a reflection of their ability to raise kids but leave your athletic accomplishments up to you. Their role in your recruiting is also as a supporting player.

The Recruiting Process can be overwhelming when coupled with the amount of work, practice, test prep and homework the average teenager has. Parents/Guardians can help with the paperwork, be the administrative assistant and lend an ear. They can, if you need it, nag you about deadlines. But colleges don't want to hear from them. You're the one who is going to be playing in college. You're the one colleges want to hear from.

How Parents/Guardians Can Help

Parents/Guardians are motivated to help you, they have the best handle on the family college budget and many times they will come up with questions that you never would have thought to ask. Keep them informed and ask for advice. You're moving on to a new challenge; think of them as a recruiting skills coach.

Adults can help you be realistic. If you've been captivated by the Steven Curry story and are set on playing Division I Basketball an adult can help you evaluate the reality of that given both your athletic and academic accomplishments.

They can help you in developing and following a Recruiting Gameplan and timeline. Frankly, most parents/guardians would rather you have Siri remind you of deadlines than go through the repercussions of nagging you about them. But they will remind you again and again if necessary. (If someone has to keep reminding you to get Athletic Recruiting chores done, you may not want to play in college as much as you think you do.)

Adults can proofread emails and correspondence for you. Everyone has a proofreader and you shouldn't be the exception. (English teachers are usually fast and efficient proofreaders and most will happily proofread for you also.) Adults should not write emails or DMs for you. It is usually very easy to spot an email written by the parent as opposed to the student-athlete and that is a big minus in your recruiting column.

Your family can help you determine your college budget. In most cases that's not something you can do on your own.   The projected average "all-in" cost of college for the 2015–2016 school year is in excess of $23,000 for state residents at public colleges, over $33,000 for out-of-state residents attending public universities, and can be over $45,000 for private universities topping out around $67,000.00.

Given these numbers, if you aren't offered a full scholarship, your family budget can be an extremely important factor in recruiting and therefore your parents/guardians really need to be involved.

The NCAA breaks sports scholarships into two categories—head count sports and equivalency sports. Students who are offered a scholarship to play a head count sport are being offered a full scholarship, while students who play equivalency sports might receive only a partial scholarship. Typically, partial scholarships range from 25% to 60% of tuition. The head count sports are all at the Division I level and include Football (D-I FBS only), Basketball (Men's and Women's), Women's Tennis,

Women's Gymnastics and Women's Volleyball. All other Division I sports are equivalency sports. Division II, NAIA and Junior Colleges also offer equivalency scholarships.

As of August 1, 2015 the NCAA changed their rules on athletic scholarships so that a DI Headcount Sport's scholarship can now cover tuition, room, board, books and fees but also the incidental costs of attending college like transportation and various personal expenses. "Cost-of-attendance scholarships" will be available in all DI sports. But, that does not mean that there are going to be a lot of cost-of-attendance scholarships given out.

If you are seeking a scholarship in an equivalency sport, generally in-state tuition is significantly less expensive than out-of-state tuition. There are states like Wyoming, South Dakota, Minnesota, New York and New Jersey that actually make it affordable for a student from another state to attend their universities so do some research on schools in those states. Also, tuition reciprocity programs between regions of the country and individual states make attending certain out-of-state institutions more affordable.

If you play baseball, softball or any of the other equivalency sports, do your homework on the "all-in" costs to attend each college you are considering. Explore the possibility of other financial aid. The athletic department at every school is intimately familiar with the options for academic scholarships, grants, student loans, etc. Most colleges have a college cost calculator on the school website that will help determine your estimated out-of-pocket costs.

Your parents/guardians can also work with you on a Camp/Combine/Showcase budget and budgets for travel or elite teams. While it might be a great adventure to go to a recruiting camp 2,000 miles away that is probably not necessary. Adults have had more experience reading through the marketing hype and getting to the genuine information so learn from them. You want to put together a 4-year budget for these expenses to have a framework of possibilities. (We deal with showcases/camps/elite teams later on in the book.)

How Adults Can Mess It Up

Parents/Guardians should not try to evaluate their athlete's talent

Most parents/guardians believe they can be objective about their athlete. That's just not true. Parents/Guardians all are going to be either too lenient in their assessment or too tough. Most don't have the breadth of experience with athletes nationwide to gauge where their own athlete's talents are on the national scale.

Parents/guardians need to find an objective source to evaluate their child's strengths and weaknesses and to give them honest feedback, especially if their assessment differs from the student-athletes.   If they don't have an honest evaluation of the athlete's talents then the college recruiting process is going to be frustrating, disappointing and littered with unexpected roadblocks.

Parents/Guardians shouldn't become the High School Coach's biggest headache

Some parents expect the high school or club coach to do all the work in the recruiting process. That's not their job. For the most part, high school coaches are paid to be full time teachers or administrators, and receive a small supplement for their added coaching responsibilities. Their time is taken. Many do a great job of promoting and guiding athletes; but it is not their responsibility to find a scholarship or roster spot for their players. Coaches will help, however student-athletes need to make it as easy for them as possible. A parent calling, emailing or trying to meet with the coach constantly takes time away from their work with their athletes and frankly becomes a pain. The athlete needs to do the legwork. The adult needs to be quiet.

Coaches do not need parents/guardians waiting to talk to them about recruiting after every practice and game. That will backfire. A high school coach's recommendation is one of the most important items on the College Coach's recruitment checklist and no College Coach wants to hear that Athlete X parents are a constant problem.

Parents/Guardians shouldn't spend the college fund on getting into college

Well-intentioned parents/guardians spend thousands of dollars every year on select teams, skills coaches, camps, showcases, videos and personal recruiters. Evaluate every dollar spent on these items. Some of these expenses are beneficial, but college recruiting doesn't have to be as expensive as we make it.

I've spoken to parents of 7th graders who are shelling out thousands on "recruiting" camps. Unless their athlete is a 1 in 1 million talent, recruiters aren't going to pay any attention to a 7'th grade Baseball player at a recruiting camp. I've known parents who ask the High School coach to let their son/daughter miss practice to go to a private coaching session. (Which is breaking the rules, being entitled and insulting the coach all in one shot.) Be selective in using specialized coaches. Be strategic when selecting camps and showcases. And don't believe that good parenting of student-athletes is measured by the amount of money you've spent.

Parents/Guardians shouldn't be a helicopter parent
Every weekend during the high school football season numerous highlight videos get sent out by parents/guardians. What that does is make the athlete look weak and unable to fend for

themselves. Those are not qualities college coaches are looking for. Being a "helicopter parent" is not healthy for your child, their team, or for you.

A parent/guardian's job is to support their athlete. That's it. They shouldn't try to be their son or daughter's coach. They shouldn't blame coaches or make excuses for undesirable outcomes. They should support their athlete's efforts to become the best teammate possible. This will go a long way toward creating a coachable, respectful, committed athlete. And that goes a long way with college coaches.

The College Coach's Perspective

At Playced we talk to College coaches often and they are generous with sharing the way their program approaches building their team. Each coach has their own method of identifying and evaluating potential athletes. Recruiting budgets and recruiting staff vary widely. But there are some constants regardless of the individual program's staff, budget, and style.

The tricky part for college programs is to project the development and maturity of a 16 or 17-year-old athlete and how successfully they will adapt to college life. Then they have to do that for several players at every position with different skill sets. They rely on numerous strategies to build the team's future.

Identifying Potential Recruits

Every coach knows the top 100 recruits in the country, but those athletes don't fill every college roster spot in America. Actually the top 100 recruits in Women's Soccer make up less than .003% of the roster spots on all college/junior college teams. The remaining roster spots are filled by projectable, coachable student-athletes.

College coaches identify potential athletes in the following ways:

1.They "beat the streets" by attending camps, showcase events and high school games to watch potential recruits compete.

2.They rely on their coaching staff, scouts and trusted personal relationships to identify athletes for their programs. They seldom listen to individuals or services with whom they are unfamiliar or who mass market athletes.

3.After signing top prospects, they fill the rest of their roster with athletes that express an interest in their program and are a good fit.

Watching film can gain a coach's interest, but nothing replaces live competition. High school and/or select games are an opportunity for a coach to see athletes play and certain reputable scouting/showcase services like Perfect Game in baseball provide an environment for college coaches to see athletes compete against the best in their sport. Recruits should take advantage of these opportunities and send their game schedule or a schedule of events they plan to attend to coaches at the colleges in which they are interested.

Player evaluation can be complicated and is certainly not an exact science. Each position, for each sport, is graded differently. For example, in football the basics are speed, agility, strength and size. Baseball coaches look for arm strength, foot speed, power and defense.

Athletes can gain valuable insight into the stats that matter in their sport by reviewing the recruiting questionnaire for their sport on any college website. This fundamental information provides an athlete with a pretty good idea of some of what a coach is looking for in his or her players.

Good statistics are not all that is necessary to play at the next level. Coaches look at more than just scouting reports. Why do you think they go to games? They want to observe a player's approach to the game, how they react to different situations, and how they interact with their coaches. Brooks Thompson, Head Men's Basketball Coach at The University of Texas at San Antonio told me:

"My coaching staff watches players from the time they step off the bus until the time they get back on the bus. We watch how they warm up, how they interact with their teammates, how they handle themselves in competition, how they win and how they lose. We evaluate the entire package; we don't just look at the box score."

And remember, character counts. College coaches want to hear words like "hard worker," "disciplined," "leader," when people talk about a potential recruit. If you don't do the hard work, if you are consistently late, have a reputation as a problem in school or don't get along with your teammates those are negatives. If you are consistently a problem for your high school coaches, that is going to count against you. When I interviewed the legendary College Football Coach Mack Brown, he told me:

"The recruits we were interested in needed to have a good relationship with their high school coach. If they couldn't have a good relationship with their high school coach, generally that spoke to their character and we would lose interest in a hurry."

8 Common Mistakes Made By Recruits

How to Avoid Common Recruiting Mistakes

Student-Athletes all tend to make similar mistakes in the recruiting process, so let's learn from their experience. These are the eight most common mistakes made by recruits.

Recruiting Mistake #1
Not contacting enough schools

To some extent your recruiting process is a numbers game. The more appropriate colleges you contact, the better your chances are to find a scholarship or a roster spot. Just because you are interested in a school doesn't mean the school will be interested in you. What if that school already has three other players at your position?

Understand that you might find that perfect fit with your first email, or it might not happen until you contact your 25th college. Everything has to line up: (1) the coach has to open your email or correspondence, (2) he or she has to actually read it, (3) there has to be a need at your position, (4) there has to be a way to verify your abilities, and (5) you have to come to an agreement.

You need to play the odds.

Recruiting Mistake #2
Having a false sense of security

Many athletes believe they are being recruited when they are not and stop working on their recruiting process. It's exciting when a college coach says they are interested in you but it just means that they are interested.

You should never have a sense of security until you sign a National Letter of Intent or have a written commitment from a school.   Keep your options open until you're certain that you have your spot.

Recruiting Mistake #3
Believing someone else will take care of your recruiting
Even though most athletes are aware that recruiting is their responsibility many still harbor the secret belief that someone else will really take care of it. Don't leave it to someone else to find your scholarship or a spot on a roster. The recruiting process is your responsibility.

College coaches want to hear from potential recruits. Your high school coach is an important contributor in your development as an athlete, they can vouch for your character and can give college coaches an honest evaluation of your abilities, but the recruiting process is still on you.

Athletes also get caught up in the "I know someone who knows the coach" syndrome. It's wonderful if your Uncle's best friend's boss plays golf with the College Coach once a week but that's not going to have any effect on the Coaches' recruiting plans. Occasionally a direct connection to a college coach might get your information looked at; you still need to be an asset to the program to get more than a look.

Recruiting Mistake #4
Waiting too long to start the process
The earlier you start the recruiting process; the more success you will have. Your window of opportunity closes with every competition that passes.

Unless you are a highly recruited athlete, you have to identify colleges to pursue, connect with the coaches and close the deal. This takes time. The sooner you get on the radar screen of the right coaches, the better off you will be and the more time you will have to evaluate which school is right for you.

If you are reading this and are already in your Junior year you are going to have to play catch-up. Start now.

Recruiting Mistake #5
Underestimating the importance of academics
If being an athlete was more important than being a student, you would be called an Athlete-Student. Many student-athletes and their parents/guardians underestimate the importance of academics in the recruiting process. College

coaches want good students, students who work hard. They don't want to worry about academic eligibility, and good students are generally highly motivated, hard-working individuals they won't have to babysit.

Recruiting Mistake #6
Spending time worrying about things you can't control

There are things that you need to be aware of but do not need to worry about. You need to know if the program you're interested in just signed three athletes who play your position, but you can't do anything about that except move them a little further down your list. Focus on what you can control and be sure you don't give the college coaches a reason to scratch you off their lists. Work hard, be a good sport, be coachable, play every game like someone is watching and don't worry if you make a mistake. These are all things you can control. Don't worry about the rest; if you do it will be a detriment to your focus and affect both grades and athletic performance.

Recruiting Mistake #7
Thinking Social Media isn't Social

Social media is not a private conversation, ever. Coaches are serious about monitoring their players' and recruits' social media activities. Their opinion of you can change with the click of "tweet." Examples abound of players getting crossed off of coaches' lists after the social media background check. Athletes have had scholarship offers withdrawn because of their social media.

> **"If you have a social media nickname or something on your Twitter account that makes me sick, I'm not going to recruit you. I've turned down players based on their Twitter handles. I've turned down players based on Twitter pictures."**
>
> Bret Bielema

One of the trends we are seeing is that, the minute a school shows interest in a recruit, alumni, fans and people who don't like you inundate the College Coaches' inbox with negative ammunition from your social media. It is not just the coaching staff who are checking. Don't give the social world anything negative to take a screenshot of.

How an athlete handles the responsibility of social media speaks to their ability to use sound judgment, to be disciplined and to recognize their responsibility as part of a team.

Recruiting Mistake #8
Targeting colleges that aren't a match
Pursuing colleges that aren't a match for you athletically and academically is a recipe for disaster. Pursuing the wrong colleges is the

most common reason that many talented athletes don't find a college team.

If you are realistic about who you are as a student and an athlete and you pursue appropriate colleges, then your recruiting journey will be a success.

Setting Goals

It's fairly common for young student-athletes to not set specific, measurable goals for where and at what level they want to play in college or goals for each year of high school. It's actually fairly common for young student-athletes to not know they need specific, measurable goals. Having clear goals is one factor we know helps success in any endeavor.

Establish your personal goals before you start the process and change them as you go if necessary.   If your goal is to play at the college level, write that down; psychology tells us that writing a goal down is much more powerful than simply thinking of your goal. Write down the specific level you want to play at and plaster it somewhere that you will see it daily. Then tell people. Give your Guidance Counselor, your coach and random strangers a heads-up. This "tell people" technique is used by some of the most successful people in the world to help keep themselves focused on their goals.

Now break your Goal into goal steps. What do you have to do each year academically to accomplish your big goal? What grades do you have to obtain in each class? What do you have to do each year athletically? What athletic skills are your weaknesses? What do you have to learn and practice to turn those into solid skills? Will you have to go to Showcases or Specific Camps? Do you have to figure out how you can afford those? Map out the smaller goal steps that lead towards your end Goal. (Like individual plays in a football game the goal steps make up the drive that gets you into the end zone.)

For each of your High School years list the Goals Steps you have to accomplish. That gives you a focus. (And it feels really good to cross off a step when it's done - there's a whole psychology behind that, but trust me, it helps keep you motivated.)

Sample Goal Chart: Grades

This is a sample of grades that you want to achieve your Freshman year if your goal is to go to College that require an average 3.0 GPA and you know that Math and Science are easier subjects for you than English and History.

Freshman Year	GPA 3.0 overall	Pt value
Eng 9	B	3
History US	B-	2.8
Alg 1	A	4
Span 2	B-	2.8
Bio1	A	4
PE	A	4
Digital Tech	B	3
		7 courses 23.6 total points 3.37 GPA

Now you have a basis to work from. If you find that Biology is giving you more trouble than you thought and you are going to get a B in that course first quarter, then you know that one of the other grades has to go up.

Academic Goals help when its 11 o'clock, you're tired and you're tempted to ditch the rest of your homework. They remind you why you're going to stay up and get it done.

Make very specific charts for your athletic accomplishments each year based on factors that you can control. Maybe you need to increase your sprint speed, or nail your serve. Those are skills that you can work on and control. You can't control being named MVP of the league or being named Athlete of the Week.

The last step before you actually start is to get a Recruiting Budget together.

Prepare a Recruiting Budget Before You Start the Process

There are many costs to consider when an athlete is serious about playing in college. Some are necessary, but many are not. If you establish a recruiting budget before you start your athletic recruiting journey and you are strategic in how you spend your money, the college recruiting process won't cost an arm and a leg. There is no reason to break into the college fund to play on the best summer team or to hire a famous speed coach. Really, there are only two categories of expenses that serious athletes have to consider – necessary costs and optional costs.

The necessary costs

Listen, if you are serious about being a college athlete you probably need to play on a summer team. Summer is the time when college coaches can attend games and tournaments. They don't have the time during their season. Playing on a summer team also shows your desire and dedication to the sport. Whether it's 7 on 7 football or club volleyball, summer is the time when you have the best chance to be seen and evaluated.

You don't have to play on the very best (or most expensive) summer team. The right team for you isn't necessarily the best team in your sport. The right team is the one with a good schedule, a good coaching staff and one where you will have an opportunity to play a significant role. While off-season play should be about exposure, it should also be about getting better. You have to play to be seen and you have to play to get better. You will accomplish neither if you are sitting on the bench while you're "playing" for the best team in the country.

When evaluating which summer team to select, keep in mind that a coach willing to help in the recruiting process is invaluable. A coach vouching for a player's abilities and character goes a long way in that player's recruiting journey.

Believe it or not, paying for and playing on a summer team is the only major cost I feel you have to incur for most sports. Obviously, having the right equipment for your sport is required, but that just goes with the territory. Depending on the sport, the cost of summer teams can range from $1,500 to $3,000, not counting the travel costs to out of town tournaments. Luckily, the rest of the major costs are optional.

If you have a limited budget or need to work during the summer, then play on a team that meets your schedule and find an inexpensive camp or two to attend on a few weekends. Do your homework on the camps and showcase events to get the biggest bang for your buck. If your recruiting budget is extremely limited, then you have to spend more time being proactive. You also have to put the work in at the gym or the field to be sure your next high school season is a success.

It doesn't cost anything to email a coach and explain your situation. If you can't afford to play for a summer team, go to the organization or team and ask for a sponsorship or set up a payment plan. You can also ask if they have a fundraising option. And, there is nothing negative about telling a coach that you have to work during the summer. Many coaches will see that as a positive and if you have stats that interest them they may have options for you.

The optional costs

The major optional costs include (but are not limited to) private lessons, showcase events, highlight videos and personal recruiters. All of these may help an athlete find a scholarship, but each one can either be managed or eliminated.

Over that last 15 years private lessons have become increasingly popular. Most instructors will charge $50 to $70 for a 30-minute session. These lessons give the athlete one-on-one time with the instructor and can help develop their skills, but $50 once or twice a week for 6 months a year can get expensive. ($50 x 2 days/week x 24 weeks = $2,400)

Your school coach or older, accomplished players are assets that you can tap into if private lessons aren't an option. Talk the situation through with your coach, they'll help you develop an alternate game plan.

Most showcase events cost $350 to $500 (before travel costs) and for that reason attending multiple camps can get expensive in a hurry. You really need to research each showcase you are considering and every tournament you are playing in. Make sure that colleges you are interested in will be attending. Be strategic with your selections and factor in playing opportunities, coaching and the potential to improve.

A highlight video can connect an athlete in Philadelphia with a coach in southern California without using up your airline miles. Most college coaches can tell if they are interested in an athlete after watching 45 seconds of video. For those two reasons, highlight videos can really be an effective recruiting tool. Just understand that the video doesn't have to be professionally produced with "The Eye of the Tiger" playing in the background. You can create an effective highlight video using your own equipment or your team's Hudl videos. Professional videos can cost from $500 to $1,500, so if you create your own video you can put that money in the college fund.

Finally, recruiting services that contact colleges on behalf of athletes might be helpful, but they are very expensive. The fees can range from $1,500 to $5,000 or more. A recruiting service is not a necessity. This is one cost that can be managed by using technology and committing to a recruiting strategy for just a few hours a month. In a recent survey of college coaches, an overwhelmingly majority of coaches DO NOT use recruiting services to find athletes and 100% of the coaches surveyed would rather hear from a recruit than a compensated recruiter.

The Season

The Work Begins

For most of you, your recruiting journey begins at the start of High School. Select sports have some recruiting going on as early as 7th grade but that's not the norm. If you're interested in playing at the next level the process starts your Freshman year. (If you are an upperclassman and have not started on your recruiting plan, don't panic. But get busy now!)

3 Commitments you have to make

Commit to being realistic

"There is a level out there for every student-athlete wanting to play at the next level! What it really boils down to is self-evaluation. If you can be honest about what kind of a player you are and what type of a student you are, you can absolutely play at the next level. It is important to identify your strengths, as well as your weaknesses when assessing what level is right for you. Being able to evaluate your own abilities, honestly, allows you to implement a game plan for your future. I strongly encourage student-athletes to approach the recruiting process with a plan. If you don't have a plan to execute, the outcome is completely out of your control." Tyrone Brooks, Director of Player Personnel for the Pittsburgh Pirates

As we've discussed, the most difficult task in an effective college recruiting game plan is being realistic with who you are as an athlete and as a student. If you spend your time pursuing colleges that aren't a fit, your recruiting experience will be a waste of time.

For high school athletes with aspirations of playing in college, there probably is a school that fits. Unfortunately, the football roster at LSU or Ohio State isn't big enough for every athlete and the academic requirements at Vanderbilt and Stanford are extremely high. For that reason, you need an objective evaluation of your abilities, both athletically and academically in order to develop a list of appropriate schools to pursue. One way to get an objective opinion would be to go to your current coach and ask him or her for an honest evaluation of your abilities. Then talk with your high school guidance counselor for an academic evaluation. Keep in mind that the evaluations might not be exactly what you want to hear, but they are perhaps the most important pieces of information you need if you want to play at the next level. You need to know which level athletic programs to pursue and you need to qualify academically to be admitted to those schools.

If the colleges that fit your evaluations aren't the ones you want to attend, then you need to work harder on the field and/or in the classroom. It is OK to pursue some dream schools, but divide your list into three groups: Stretch schools, realistic schools and fall back schools. Pursue each school in the same way. You might be surprised how much more attractive a college becomes when they want you on their team. Also remember that just because you haven't heard about a school, that doesn't mean it isn't a perfect match for you. You might be pleasantly surprised.

Commit to the process
Committing to the process means taking ownership of your college search. You have to put in your time. You have to be involved and proactive. Being proactive means reaching out to the coaches at the colleges in which you have interest in and developing a dialogue with them. It means doing the work even when you're really tired and don't particularly want to.

Don't try to hand the process off to someone else and hope they'll do a great job for you. It's not their future.

Commit to being persistent
The commitment to being persistent does not mean writing one email to a few college coaches or putting one video up on a recruiting platform and then waiting for the scholarship offers to roll in the door. Understand that your initial contact with a coach is an introduction and you likely aren't going to land a roster spot with one email.

In fact, it might take many attempts before you hear anything back from them at all.

You really need to contact numerous schools, numerous times to find the right fit. No matter how you connect with college coaches everything has to line up to get a response: (1) the coach has to open your email or letter, (2) he or she has to actually read it, (3) there has to be a need at your position. (4) there has to be a way to verify your abilities, and (5) you have to come to an agreement. For that reason, to some extent your recruiting process is a numbers game. The more appropriate colleges you reach out to, the better your chances are to find a roster spot or scholarship. You might find that perfect fit with your first email, or it might not happen until you contact your 25th college.

You need to get your mental game in place with recruiting. When a college coach isn't interested in you don't take it personally. That isn't necessarily a comment on your ability, your character, or your chances to play in college. It just means that you don't fit their roster needs. Don't let disinterest or rejection discourage you; you're an athlete, you know that being behind on the scoreboard doesn't mean you're going to lose the game.

Your Recruiting Timeline: A Year-By-Year Approach

Freshman Year   Freshman Year Checklist

	Set Your Goals. Put your Goals List in a place you see it every day
	Plan High School Courses for 4 years
	Learn the Amateur Rules
	Learn to Use Social Media as an Athlete
	Get the Grades
	Research Colleges and Universities
	Develop a Favorites list of Colleges and Universities
	Research Showcases and Camps/Combines
	Develop a Favorites list of Showcases and Camps/Combines
	Develop a plan for Elite/Club teams
	Begin stockpiling video clips and pictures

Set Your Goals

We've been through some goal setting. At the beginning of your freshman year review your goals for the year. Review the grades you have set as goals in each course. Review the athletic skills you need to strengthen. Make any modifications at the beginning of the year and then don't change the list. Goals aren't goals if they fluctuate when things get a little tough.

Get the Grades

Freshman year can be a period of adjustment but your grades can't slide. If you have trouble with a course, ask for help immediately and get back on track quickly. There are also great online free resources for most subjects.

A low GPA your Freshman year puts tremendous pressure on you during the rest of your high school career. If you hope to be an NCAA DI bound athlete, there is that new rule that "locks" course grades after your 6th semester so you can't retake a course your Senior year and have that count in your overall Core GPA. That means that a lower grade in a Freshman class can put you in summer school before your Junior year, which is not the way you want to spend summer.

You also need to remain eligible to play at your High School. Eligibility is generally determined by state athletic associations, which often allow the individual school districts to impose higher academic eligibility requirements.   So, for example, Texas has state standards for public education which includes the rule that you can't have any failures in any course in order to be eligible to play, but Texas also allows each district to impose **higher** eligibility standards. There are some states where you can fail a class as long as you maintain an acceptable average GPA. (Although you probably can't meet NCAA requirements that way!) Know the grades you need to maintain in order to stay eligible to play your sport.

In some schools there are Athletic Academic coordinators who oversee Athlete Eligibility. These are usually coaches who are also teachers. If you find that you are totally lost in a course or having more trouble with a subject than you anticipated, and you have an Athletic Academic Coordinator, seek them out. They're a great resource.

Know the Amateur Rules

 If you have any doubt about your amateur status talk to your Guidance Counselor and Coach about "amateur status."

Most states require that an athlete who is part of their High School program be classified as an "amateur." You must be an amateur to qualify to play in college. That pretty much means that you can't get paid for playing or being good at your sport, endorsing a product or company as an athlete, or accepting gifts given because of your athletic ability. It also means that you can't play on a team of professionals, although you can play on a team that includes professional athletes if you don't get paid to play. There are a lot of shades of this rule and you want to discuss your particular situation with the people who know the rules.

If you and your coach are still uncertain about whether a team or opportunity would hurt your amateur status, call the NCAA Eligibility Center team. They are extremely helpful and glad to talk to you. (877/262-1492)

Learn to Use Social Media

I know, you've been using Social Media since you could tap a mobile phone. But now you need to use Social Media as an athlete, as a public person.   Coaches will use your social media as a background check. In fact, they use your Social feeds to help determine if you fit their team culture. There are numerous stories of recruits who have been crossed off of "possible" lists based solely on their social media.

Programs like Southern Methodist University have shared part of their social media analysis of players, which includes a detailed analysis of language, pictures and also retweets of SMU information.

The majority of sports are looking to social media as a way to get to know the person the athlete is beyond the playing venue. Understand and take into account that nothing in social media is actually private; screen shots of "private" conversations and photos find their way into College Coaches in-boxes with regularity. Coaches have withdrawn offers due to an athlete's social media. And, unlike a lot of the factors in recruiting, you have complete control over your feeds.

As you go through your high school experience remember that almost everyone has video capability and will use it.
Follow the programs you are hoping to play for on social media. Start sharing their information; regardless of how many followers/fans a program has the people who consistently share out information are eventually noticed. Decide on the rules on social for your "brand;" then follow those rules.

Plan High School Courses
Determine which courses you need and when you have to take them.

Make a chart of all the courses you need to take during your High School Career and which years you have to take each course in your school's curriculum path. Take into account NCAA/NAIA eligibility, the requirements of the schools you are interested in, and your High School graduation requirements.

Some schools have pre-requisites for courses and some have restrictions on the number of students accepted into a particular course each year. Once you have your chart, sit down with your Guidance Counselor and map out a practical path. If you're aiming for an NCAA school, check the courses you'll be taking on the NCAA site to be certain the courses qualify. (https://web3.ncaa.org/hsportal/exec/hsAction?hsActionSubmit=searchHighSchool)

Research Colleges and Universities and Develop a Favorites List
The recurring theme of recruiting wisdom is "be realistic." That's hard to do when you're a Freshman and both physically and skill-wise you have a lot of growing to do. Physically you have to guess. Want to play DI Basketball but are stuck at 5'9"? Your physician, based on your growth history and family history can help you guess at your height Senior year. If the conclusion is that you're not going to grow much above 5'11" then you won't be playing the post at UCLA. It doesn't mean that you absolutely can't play DI, just that you aren't going to physically fit into what those programs traditionally look for. There are "Cinderella" stories in every sport, so keep your dream schools on the list but spend the majority of your time on more realistic alternatives. (None of the

big programs wanted Steven Curry, the NBA's MVP; Davidson did pretty well by him.)

You have more control over mastering the skills you need. Here's a place where you also need to be realistic and honest with yourself. If you love your sport, play it pretty well, don't want to spend the hours each day that it takes to excel but want to play in college, then don't look to colleges that have high level, intensely competitive programs. If you are determined to play in a high level program your high school experience is going to be different than a lot of your peers; you'll be spending more of your time investing in your athletic future. Know that and make a decision that's right for you.

You need to take your academics into account too. If you are a good student but don't foresee putting in the time to be a great student you probably shouldn't put any of the Ivy League schools on your "practical" list. If you are in an academically competitive high school, you have an advantage; colleges know which high schools are academically "tough." If you are not, you need to let your grades and Standardized Test scores do the talking.

Make a list of the schools that match your abilities and preferences or use the Playced Matching technology to generate a list. The list probably will change somewhat over your high school years and that's normal; this is a starting point.

Research Showcases and Camps

"…showcases are far from equal when it comes to exposure." Jerry Ford, President Perfect Game

Large high school programs that have consistent media coverage give you an advantage in "being known" and the goal is to be known before you are needed. If you live in a smaller town and go to a small school it is a harder to get noticed; recruiting will take a little more effort. For student-athletes in schools that don't get a lot of attention, you want to try to schedule in showcases and camps so that you have some additional exposure; just do your research and be certain the showcases or camps/combines attract coaches from programs you are interested in. (Refer to your Favorite College list.) You may not want to attend these until later in High School when your sports skills have matured, especially if you have limited funding for showcases and camps. Remember you only have one shot at making a first impression on college coaches.

Showcase, camp and combine formats differ based on the sport you play. But for all you want to be certain that:

The program is established and has a good reputation.

The Organizer/Company running the event can be the difference between a totally disorganized jumble and a real chance to show your skills. Connect on social media with athletes who have been to camps and get their feedback. If an organization is just putting their brand on the event, find out who is actually running it. Finally, check the Better Business Bureau's listing to be sure the Organizers don't have a long list of complaints; some companies do.

Insurance

While you assume that the company sponsoring the showcase/combine has insurance for the event, if your own insurance coverage is minimal and your school insurance doesn't cover outside events you may want to check on what insurance options the camp/showcase has available.

Check The Venue

You also want to check that the courts or field are well cared for. Some organizations play on horribly maintained surfaces; that's a recipe for injury.

If you are accustom to playing on turf and the venue is grass that is a great learning experience and should be looked at that way. But if you are trying to impress a college coach, a change in surface might not be what you want.

Check that Athletic Trainers or Medical Personnel will be present

There are events, especially one day Combines, that don't have an athletic trainer in sight. You want to factor that in, along with your own injury history when you decide on an event.

The overall price of the program should be reasonable

Check what the price of the event includes and whether there are add-ons which you have to pay for. Calculate the cost of traveling to and from the event and food and lodging if necessary. Then decide if the potential benefit of going to the camp justifies the cost.

Refund policy

Find out if there is a way to get your money back if you are injured or have a family emergency prior to the camp. Things happen that are out of your control. Know what the refund policy is for the camp/combine/showcase that you are going to.

Which College Coaches are expected?

No event organizer can guarantee that specific coaches will be at the camp, combine or showcase. Even Coaches who expect to attend can have circumstances come up that make it impossible for them to get there. But the event organizer should be able to produce a list of coaches who are expected to be there.

The exception is if a camp is at a college and run by the college coaches. You're pretty much guaranteed that they'll be there.

Take into account the size of the Event
How many athletes are participating? Depending on your sport and your previous exposure the number of athletes at the camp or showcase counts.   Coaches can only watch so many athletes over the course of a day, but they also probably aren't going to travel to a very small camp unless they know they want to watch a particular athlete.

If there are going to be hundreds of players there, what is your playing time going to be? Some events will put you on the field long after college coaches are in their cars on the way to the next event.

It is simply unrealistic to believe that a coach can watch and evaluate every athlete and they certainly can't be at every game. College coaches have to be efficient, so they spend their time watching the athletes on their list. Therefore, the key is to get on as many lists as possible. To do that takes a little preparation. If the coaches don't know your name when they arrive and you don't have a plan, they probably will not know your name when they leave.

Reach out to the coaches at those schools you're interested prior to going to the recruiting camp or showcase. Provide them with a link to your video, some information on your athletic abilities, your academic achievements and the contact information for your current coach. At least that way they know your name before they arrive. Then, follow up with the college coaches shortly after the event.

Check with your High School Coach
Coaches know a lot that isn't public information. Before you pay for a camp, combine or showcase, ask your coach if it's a good idea.

Develop a plan for Elite/Club Teams
These decisions are again, based on your sport, the strength of your high school program and what your goal schools are. You also have to take time, expense, and transportation into account. Remember that your academics are incredibly important so if playing on a Club team is going to mean you don't have time to get decent grades then opt for the academics.

For sports like Football and there are few "Elite" teams, you're looking at 7v7 and Fall Ball/Indoor as the additional options. For sports like Basketball, elite teams are the norm. Volleyball and Soccer thrive on Club teams. Baseball /Softball also make use of Club/Elite teams. That does not mean that the best team is the most expensive. There are numerous programs which don't cost a lot and it's your job to seek them out.

Talk to the people who play for the teams and listen objectively before you try out or join. This decision isn't about which team your best friend is playing on, it's about which team works best for you.

You have to fit into the Elite team roster and you have to be able to play. There are a lot of club teams who have very full benches and if you end up on the bench that doesn't help you develop in your sport. A Club/Elite team coach is not going to promise you a specific amount of playing time because circumstances change but they should be able to tell you the percent of time each player usually plays.

Coaching should focus on teaching and the coaches should promote athletic development. The coaching staff of a travel, elite or club team should also be willing to be references for you with college coaches.

You want to take basic practicalities into account. Be sure that you are spending your time wisely. Travelling two hours to practice several days a week can exhaust you.

Exhausted athletes are more prone to injury and less prone to doing well academically.

Overuse injuries are another consideration in playing your sport year round for a club or elite team. We know that playing the same sport year round can be harmful to the growing athlete. We know that an overuse injury can sideline athletic careers. We also know that many college coaches prefer multi-sport athletes. A lot of Elite athletes peg their success on the fact they played multiple sports in high school; Amy Wambach attributes her soccer success to playing basketball at the high school level. In his Hall of Fame speech, pitcher John Smoltz warned:

"I want to encourage the families and parents that are out there that this is not normal to have a surgery at 14 and 15 years old. That you have time, that baseball is not a year-round sport. That you have an opportunity to be athletic and play other sports. Don't let the institutions that are out there running before you guaranteeing scholarship dollars and signing bonuses that this is the way…."

So before you decide to play your sport year round because it's what "everyone" does, take academics, time, expenses, lack of diverse skills and potential injury into account.

Start an Athletic Resume & Video Archive

Your athletic resume should be a working document, one that you add to after every event. You can take the details out when you are ready to finalize it, but you'd be surprised at the important points of your play that you forget.

You also want to start accumulating video to eventually make into highlight and/or skills recruiting videos.

If your school videotapes games, ask if you can use a copy of the video in your recruiting. If it's not possible to use school video, plan who is going to take video for you and how often so you don't have a great game and realize that no one filmed it.

Being organized from the beginning will save you tremendous time in the long term. The extra 60 seconds it takes to write down a highlight of a game or label a video or picture correctly will save a lot of frustration when it comes time to put everything together.

Video, once exclusively used for football, is increasingly becoming a way to highlight your skills in numerous sports. It serves as a virtual handshake to any college coaching staff in the country; it's just easier for a coach to be interested in you if they can see a slice of your playing performance. Video was also once the realm of people who could afford expensive cameras or whose coach had events filmed. Today good quality video can be produced by most 10 year olds.

"Discovery is the name of the game when it comes to college recruiting. Every year we hear about college coaches finding athletes because of their highlight reel. This applies to all levels and every sport. Whether you want to play DI or DIII, a highlight reel can get you in front of recruiters. Quite simply, video has the ability to connect the right players with the right coaches." Erik Pulverenti, General Manager of Media for Hudl

Videos and pictures should be labeled and the dated. Initially save images/videos in a folder on your phone then transfer them to separate folders on the cloud or back them up on a laptop/desktop or removable hard drive and add them as "unlisted" in your YouTube account. Phones get damaged, or ruined and you don't want to lose all of your highlights if you phone meets an untimely demise.

Be consistent in labelling your media. If you have to go back your Junior year and ferret out important clips you're giving yourself a major headache; there's no sense in making the process harder.

Freshman Home-Schooled Athletes

A note if you are Home-Schooled or will be Home-Schooled for any part of your High School career; there are specific criteria for Home Schooled student-athletes for both the NCAA and NAIA.

NCAA Home Schooled
http://www.ncaa.org/student-athletes/future/home-school-students

The NAIA considers their eligibility criteria met for Home Schooled students who have a minimum 20 on the ACT or a combined 950 on the SAT Math & Verbal.
▯

Sophomore Year Sophomore Checklist

	Register with the NCAA Eligibility Center
	Take the PSAT
	Research how coaches in your sport evaluate athletes
	Set up a meeting with your Coaches
	Discuss the family college budget with your parents/guardians.
	Update your Favorites List
	Check that you're on track with your High School courses
	Review your Skills Development Plan
	Continue building your Athletic Resume
	Send initial contact emails to Coaches on your Favorites List

Register

Register with the NCAA Eligibility Center if you're interested in NCAA schools. (Just a note: as of this writing NCAA registration does not work well on a lot of mobile phones. Head for a laptop when you register with the Eligibility Center.) You can't register with the NAIA until after your Junior year (early determination) or at the end of your Senior year.

Sorry about this one - Take the PSAT

Take the PSAT to determine where you stand. If you are not a comfortable test- taker think of the PSAT as a pre-season match or game.

Standardized tests like the PSAT, SAT and ACT try to evaluate how well you will do academically at the college level, period. Some brilliant people do very poorly on these tests initially, some great students do better on the ACT than the SAT, and some excellent prospects are more comfortable with the SAT format. The PSAT is a baseline for you to use to decide how you're going to work towards doing well on the actual SAT or ACT, and you will need to do well because one of those tests are required for both NCAA and NAIA eligibility.

Before you take the PSAT, take a few of the free sample tests, just to get a sense of the "competition "rules. The sample tests also have a separate document you can download that

explains why the correct answers are the correct answers and that is really helpful.
https://collegereadiness.collegeboard.org/pdf/psat-nmsqt-practice-test-1.pdf

If a test-prep course is not offered at your high school and a private course is out of reach, there are DIY options. (Or if your schedule is so tight that you need to only work online.) Both the ACT site and the SAT site offer sample tests, daily questions and strategies. Khan Academy has a free SAT prep course which is personalized for you and is as much fun as a test prep course can be. https://www.khanacademy.org/test-prep/sat

Online Sites like SparkNotes have free ACT strategies and sample tests
http://www.sparknotes.com/testprep/books/act

Once you get your scores back decide what you have to concentrate on for the actual SAT or ACT and make space in your schedule to do that work.

Learn How Your Sport Evaluates Athletes
Each sport evaluates its athletes differently. Understanding how you are going to be evaluated is just a matter of settling in and doing the work. Re-searching does, in this instance, mean searching again and again. There are some common skills that the majority of coaches

in a sport look for in a position, in addition some programs look at other metrics or intangibles to evaluate talent. You are going to have to dig, just asking Siri what college volleyball coaches are evaluating in recruits isn't going to do it.

Listen to the press conferences coaches in your sport give in the pre-season. What they praise in their new players are qualities they are looking for. Carefully read the articles where coaches are asked about their new recruits. For example, for defensive players Volleyball coaches are not only looking for controlled passes and digs but for quickness, balance and excellent body control. The chart below gives the very general skill sets college coaches will look for in several sports. This is the kind of information you want for your own sport.

ATHLETIC FACTORS

In baseball, a positional player's abilities are measured by arm strength, speed, power, batting average and defense. Pitchers are graded on velocity, movement, control and potential.

Coaches are also looking for intangibles; for things that can't be measured with a scale or stopwatch. Intangibles are the attributes an athlete possesses or the behavior he or she exhibits that don't require talent, but are crucial to success. These intangibles are sometimes difficult to measure, but they can be the difference maker when a coach is trying to decide between two athletes of similar abilities.

One intangible coaches in every sport always look at is your work ethic. Follow any elite player and you will find that they work tremendously hard; that's one of the character traits coaches want to hear when people talk about you.

Set Up A Meeting With Your Coaches
Meet with your coach to review his or her assessment of your abilities. Listen objectively, as if you are listening to a summary of someone else's skills and abilities. Take notes or, if it is

okay with your coach, record the conversation on your mobile. It is sometimes difficult to focus on the most important points during a conversation. Then ask specific questions. If your coach says you need to be faster, that's a broad statement. See if they can give you a specific example so you can work on the skills that will make you faster in the situations they are talking about.

A caveat here, your coach's assessment is a general guideline. They are judging your abilities in the context of the kids they have coached and their experience in the sport, so the strength of the program may make a difference in the assessment you get. You want to balance the coach's assessment and your own determination. Michael Jordan didn't make the varsity roster his sophomore year while fellow sophomore Leroy Smith did. I am not sure how far Leroy's basketball career went, but it doesn't compare to Jordan's. World Cup Champion and Golden Ball winner Carli Llyod was cut from the under-21 national team in 2003 and almost quit the sport completely. The point is that Coaches are judging your skills at the moment and your effort at this moment. You can change that assessment for better or worse in the next few years.

.

How Your Coach Can Help

Here is a typical first conversation between a student-athlete and his or her coach about recruiting:

Athlete: "Coach, I really want to play in college. Are you willing to help me out?"

Coach: "Sure, do you have any ideas on where you want to play?"

Athlete: "Not really. I just want to keep playing."

Coach: "How are your grades?"

Athlete: "Pretty good."

Coach: "Do you know what you want to study?"

Athlete: "No, but I'm pretty good in math."

Coach: "Do you want to stay close to home? Does the size of the school matter to you?"

Athlete: "I don't care. I just want to play."

What in the world is a coach going to do with that information?

Most coaches want to see their athletes make it to the next level, but you have to help them help you. First and foremost, do not ask them to contact colleges that aren't a match for your abilities. Make sure they agree with the schools you want to pursue. Then give them the specific information they need to effectively help you:

1. Your Athletic resume
2. Your Academic resume
3. A list of potential colleges and coach contact information.

Discuss the Family College Budget

As I've said, most athletic scholarships are partial scholarships, so budget is a factor in determining which colleges you pursue. Let's repeat that, most athletic scholarships are partial scholarships. Only NCAA I football, men's and women's basketball, tennis, gymnastics and women's volleyball offer full rides to athletes who have been chosen to receive athletic scholarships. (That does not apply to Ivy League Schools who don't offer Athletic Scholarships; their financial packages make up for that.) So if you're a soccer player it's highly unlikely you're going to get a full scholarship.

Remember that the NCAA DII and NAIA models are usually combinations of athletic scholarships, grants, financial aid, and work-study. And, any athletic scholarship is for one year; they're not guaranteed for four years. (NCAA DI has a ruling that athletic scholarships can't be withdrawn due to athletic play but they can be withdrawn for other reasons.) You have to earn your scholarship money every year.

Also, look into schools like Duke University who meet the demonstrated financial need of every student. Schools whose admissions are "need-blind", accept applicants based on their merits,

regardless of their ability to pay for college, and their financial aid department works with the student to work out the finances; so if you're accepted you will be able to go.
Consider the tuition benefits of in-state schools as you plan.

Before you update your potential college list you want a realistic picture of whether that school is a practical one for you, your academic and athletic abilities, and your financial resources.

Update Your Favorite Colleges List
Update your "Favorites" List of the 20-30 colleges you realistically qualify for. Take another look at your "stretch" schools. Do another check on the entrance requirements of those schools; the schools may require courses beyond the core courses the NCAA requires or your school requires for graduation. For example, NCAA DI and DII Eligibility does not have a foreign language requirement: Ohio State requires 2 years of a foreign language, Princeton requires 4 years of 1 foreign language and Oregon State requires a minimum or 2 years of one foreign language or a satisfactory score on an approved foreign language test. Now you need to take another look at the courses you have mapped out for the next few years and be certain that you are meeting each college's requirements as well as the Athletic Eligibility requirements.

Check that you are on track with your courses

Use the NCAA Division I core course worksheet to make sure you are on track with the core course requirements. Review your 4-year plan and make any necessary changes based on new interests or courses that you've decided you want to take.

Review your Skills Development and Plan

Sometimes you can turn a weakness into a strength quickly and sometimes it is frustratingly slow. Review your chart of athletic strengths and weaknesses. Modify your plan according to your real progress.

Keep in mind that repeating a movement incorrectly is not going to help; that will only reinforce the wrong movement. Ask for help. Your coaches can often spot exactly what you are doing wrong and pinpoint methods of correcting that.

Continue Building Your Athletic Resume

Add videos, pictures, and media coverage to your resume. That media coverage doesn't have to spotlight you; it can be about your team. Articles about anything that your team does on and off the field should be filed.

I'm going to add, again, be organized! It really will save you a ton of trouble later on.

Send Initial Contact Emails to Coaches on Your Favorites List

Tips for an effective first email

Once you've finished reviewing your list of Favorite Colleges, send the coaches an introductory email.   There is no recipe for writing your initial email, but here are some tips that should help:

- Use your research to personalize your message. I can't emphasize this enough; personalize your emails.

-The subject line of your email should make the coach want to open it. For example, "1st Team All District Quarterback" or "Power Forward averaging 12.2 rebounds per game."

-Your salutation should be to the specific coach by name (Dear Coach Smith).

-Introduce yourself as a potential candidate for his or her program.

-Provide academic information: ACT or SAT score, GPA, class rank, honors, etc.

-Provide athletic information: position, height, weight, honors, and relevant statistics.

-Provide a link to your video (if you have one).

-Include a current game schedule with dates, locations and times.

-Include the contact information for your high school and summer coaches.

-Include your contact information (email, cell, home address).

-Include a brief statement of why you think you would benefit their program.

College coaches really want to hear from you. Most programs have a limited recruiting budget and they can only focus on a particular geographic area to observe potential recruits so if you aren't in that area, they may never see you. A compelling email and a link to your highlight video might open the door for many coaches who know nothing about you.

Junior Year Junior Checklist

	Update your Favorites List
	Check your High School Courses
	Prepare for & take the SAT or ACT
	Create a Highlight Video
	Clean up your Social Media
	Meet with Your Guidance Counselor
	Meet with Your Coach
	Schedule/Take Unofficial Visits
	Prepare a list of Questions to ask College Coaches
	Prepare for questions College Coaches might ask you
	Attend Camps/Combine/Showcases that make sense
	Keep in Contact with Coaches who have contacted you
	Get Financial Aid in Order
	Get Your Mental Game in order

Junior Year

Updates

Review and update your Favorite Colleges list. Make any changes that you need to based on your academics, athletics, and budget situation. For any new entries contact the college coaches.

Use the NCAA Division I core course worksheet to make sure you are on track with the core course requirements. Use your Admissions Requirements Chart from sophomore year to be certain that you've still got the necessary courses in your plan.

Prepare for and take the SAT or ACT

You want to give yourself time to retake the test if you're not happy with your scores so you should normally take the test during your Junior year.

Fee waivers are available but have to be processed through your Guidance Counselor or School Administration which takes time. For that reason, you need to give your Guidance Department the necessary information at the beginning of this year.

When you register for the SAT you can chose to send scores to four places. (There is a fee to send scores after these 4 choices or if you ask they be sent any time 9 days after the actual test.) You can also sign up for Score Choice which lets you decide after you see your scores if you want them sent out.

When you register for the SAT you can opt in to their Student Search Service, a free service which some colleges use to search for suitable applicants; they will send you materials if they do have interest in you. If a college is interested in you as a student that's a great way to start an email introducing yourself to a coach. It's simply one other tentacle out there in that recruiting sea but it's free and it only takes 10 minutes so you might as well fill it out.

The ACT offers the ACT profile which is free. It's a tech tool that helps you decide which careers (and majors) you're best suited for.

Note: the ACT requires a current photo to be submitted when you register for the test. That photo will print on your ticket and on the score report that is automatically sent to your high school.

9999 is the code to have your SAT scores sent to the NCAA Eligibility Center. Only test scores sent from the College Board (SAT) are accepted; you can't have your Guidance Counselor send the scores.

9876 is the code to have your SAT scores or ACT scores sent to the NAIA Eligibility Center.

Create a Highlight Video

Highlight videos and game film used to strictly be used for football, but they have become very important in the ever-competitive world of college recruiting for many sports.

Video alone may not land you a scholarship or roster spot, but it certainly will serve as a virtual handshake to any college coaching staff in the country. What could be a better introduction to a college coach than an honest, unbiased evaluation of your abilities? Video doesn't lie and it doesn't have an opinion.

As I said earlier, a highlight video does not have to be professionally produced. Coaches are looking for your athletic abilities not your film-making prowess.

Guidelines for Highlight Videos

•Keep it short; two or three minutes is long enough. A coach is going to decide if he or she is interested in you during the first 45 seconds.

•Because the coach is going to make a determination during the first 45 seconds or so, **put your best highlights first**. Athletes have a tendency to put highlights in chronological order - don't. You only get one chance at a first impression; you want your most impressive play or skill to be the first thing the coach sees.

•Make the video with the coaches of your sport in mind. Different sports require different approaches. For example, baseball and softball coaches would generally rather see video of your skills than game footage. Sports like basketball and football are the opposite, the coaches want to see game footage.

•If you have different skills you want to showcase, don't be afraid to create more than one highlight video. Let's repeat that, there is a general belief that you can only have one highlight video. You can have several, a general video and others that are specific to certain skills. Most platforms allow multiple videos for each player.

•Showcase all your skills and use clips that show you're a well-rounded athlete.

•Use spot shadows or arrows when necessary to help the viewers find you on the film. Don't overuse them though, that interferes with being able to see the actual skills or plays.

•If you are putting statistics in text on the video, put in your real statistics. I can't tell you how many times we see student-athletes who claim to have run the 40yd dash in 4.3. That's a good NFL Combine time. If you actually are that fast as a 16-year-old, then tag the time with the verifier. If you don't have stellar stats, that's okay; coaches value honesty and they value progress.

•Video Quality is Important. Sounds like I'm contradicting what I just told you about not having to use a professional, doesn't it? But we're talking about clarity and ease of viewing when we say video quality is important.

After you've made your highlight video, upload it to YouTube or Vimeo; add the Highlight Video as the Featured Video on your Facebook page. Include the video link in any correspondence you have with college coaches.

And remember that a general highlight video can be changed.   If you've had a great game or competition and want to substitute a clip from that into your Highlights, you can do that. Consider it a work in progress.

Clean up your Social Media
Every recruit needs to take a careful look at their "Tweets and Replies" and remove Tweets and Retweets that are offensive. Although "delete" doesn't mean that there isn't a screen shot in someone's archive, at least you've made an effort to re-evaluate your feeds.   Take the pictures off of Instagram that you thought were hysterically funny when you were 13 but are inappropriate. Remove everything that is inappropriate, illegal or just plain stupid.

On Twitter, request your Archive so you have a total view of what coaches and their staff will be looking at. (Go to your profile picture in the upper right hand corner and click "Settings" from the Drop Down Menu. Scroll to the bottom of that page and click "Request Your Archive." Twitter will email it to you.) For Instagram go through every photo; when a coaching staff checks your Instagram account, they are going to check it all.

On Facebook you want to be certain that your cover photo relates to your sport, we process visuals 60,000 times faster than text and Facebook's cover photo is large and prominent. That photo will stick in people's minds.

We know that you wouldn't be reckless enough to have a drop box where you share photos with friends, so there's no need to tell you to get rid of it- right?

Review your progress with your Guidance Counselor
Meet with your Guidance Counselor to review your courses and GPA. Your Guidance Counselor has more paperwork to do for student-athletes than for the majority of their college bound students so make it as easy for them as you can. You should have your Favorite College List, ask for their input and add colleges they suggest to your list of schools to research.

Check that your transcripts have been sent to the NCAA prior to the meeting and rectify the situation if they haven't arrived.

Some high schools have Guidance Personnel, Coaching Academic Advisors, or Teacher-Coaches who are experts in the student-athlete recruiting process. If there are experts available, take advantage of their knowledge.

Ask your coach to assess your abilities
Meet with your coach to review his or her assessment of your abilities. Before you go into the meeting list questions that you want to ask. First, listen carefully to what your coach has to say. Then ask questions. Use the answers to modify your plans if necessary.

Ask if they have any suggestions as far as colleges go. Your coach may have a college program in mind that you haven't considered.

Get your coach involved as a reference
Remember it's not the coach's job to find you a college home, it's your job. Ask him or her if they would reach out to your 5 favorite colleges. You are going to give your coaches your athletic resume, video links and the contact information for the coaches at each college. Beside the contact information write a line defining who this college coach is and their position. The easier you make it for your coach, the more they will be

able to be involved and use their time effectively to help you.

Review and update your list of colleges
 Maintain a Favorites List of 20-30 colleges at levels you realistically qualify for. Have your "reach" schools on a sub-list.

At this point you can probably subtract a couple of colleges from your sophomore list and possibly add a few. You will have a better sense of who you are as a student, as a player and what the colleges' rosters are going to look like.

Go on Unofficial Visits
Schedule and take two or three unofficial visits to colleges that have expressed an interest in you and that you're interested in.

Unofficial visits are visits you pay for, so don't go to look at schools you aren't seriously interested in. The majority of High Schools allow time off for college visits without penalty but there is also generally a limit to how many you may take and you need to go through the paperwork. Give the college and coach sufficient notice that you're coming; you should be able to meet with the coach as long as you're not in a Dead Period if it's an NCAA school. Remember to use some common sense in scheduling. If you schedule your visit during the week before the biggest game of the season, the coach isn't going to have a lot of extra time for anyone and may not be able to talk to you at all.

Prepare questions to ask college coaches during your unofficial visit
First, before you meet with a coach, know what you can about the program, the school and the school's requirements. It is insulting to the Coach to take up time asking basic questions that are answered on the College website or athletic page. The last thing you want to do is insult the person who may hold a key to your future.

Before you meet you should know the information on their athletic department website the way you know your own playbook. It is quickly apparent if you're asking questions whose answers are publically available and no one is going to believe you are interested in a program if you haven't bothered to go through the basics. (That goes for phone/Skype/Messenger "meetings" also.)

Regardless of the communication method, coaches want to get to know you, get a feel for your personality, and determine what kind of person you are – so be your "on my best behavior" self.

Coaches expect you to ask questions. For most of us, the one question we really want the answer to is the one we forget to ask once we're in an interview, so write the questions down or put them in notes on your mobile. Take the list into the meeting with you. Coaches appreciate that you have thought carefully about their program and have specific questions.

One thing you do want is to know is what the Coach expects from their players and their team off the field. Some programs have dry seasons and enforce that. Some programs have athlete's dining rooms or tables and expect you to follow the sports nutritionist's guidelines. You want to know what is expected of you as a member of the team beyond just your sport participation.

Other questions you might want to ask the Coach:
Are there team/athletic study halls/tutoring?
How are conflicts between academics and athletics handled? If the team travels and there is a test while the team is out of town what is the procedure for testing?
What are the summer obligations with the program?

What kind of players succeed here?

What would I need to do to earn a scholarship to your program?

How many players do you project you'll recruit at my position/specialty in my graduation year?

What would I need to do to be formally evaluated by your staff?

Finally, ask what else the coach needs from you and what the procedure is from this point on.

Prepare for questions a coach might ask

Coaches are going to ask you about any red flags in your file or on your social media. Be ready to answer truthfully and explain what an incident taught you. If you were an idiot when you were a freshman, have an answer ready that concisely explains how you turned that around. If you aren't a visual person and didn't do tremendously well in an Art class be ready to explain that it was a requirement and you did as well as you'd expect yourself to do grade wise.

Coaches are probably going to ask you why you want to play for their program. That's a complex question so think about the answer and refine it. List the points that make the program and college attractive. List the points that make you believe you will fit into the program and that the program fits you. Then actually "write" out the answer. Once you have the answer coherently in your mind, you will be able to articulate your reasons to the coach.

Expect to be asked: "Who is helping you with this decision?" For many coaches this will be one of the first questions asked. They want to know who will be influential in making the decision and who to build a relationship with. I believe a recruit should limit the number of people involved in the process. Listen to your parents, your current coach and perhaps a trusted advisor. Don't poll the team, or ask the cashier at the grocery store. This is your decision and coaches don't enjoy having to work with several people to sign a recruit.

Coaches are also usually going to ask what your strengths and weaknesses as a player are. This is not the time to be modest. Be humble, but confident in your abilities. If you can give specific examples, you should. Know your stats, so you can share them with coaches without looking them up. College coaches want self-confident, outgoing players that will represent their school in the right way. Be honest about your weaknesses, but don't dwell on them. They know you aren't perfect and likely will prefer an athlete that recognizes areas where they need to improve.

A question that is generally asked during an interview is: "What sets you apart from other recruits?" The answer to this question is different for every athlete, but if you have a strong answer it can go a long way toward earning a college roster spot or scholarship. Some qualities you could highlight in answering this question might be leadership, work ethic, academic achievements, coachability, mental toughness, and sportsmanship. If you are involved in programs outside of school, be sure to mention them. If you've overcome difficulties in your personal life and see your resilience as a strength, tell them.

Anyone in sports is a competitor and College Coaches fit that profile. A coach is going to ask about the other colleges that are recruiting you. If you are being recruited by other colleges, let them know, but you need to be clear that their school is one of your top choices. If you aren't currently being recruited, there are many ways to answer this question. For example, you could say "I have just started the process" or "I am waiting to hear back from several colleges."

The coach will generally ask you what type of scholarship/financial aid you are looking for. Let the coach know if you have other offers on the table. Be honest about financial considerations, especially if that is a determining factor in your ultimate decision. If partial scholarships are the norm in your sport, be open to other forms of financial aid including academic scholarships, grants and student loans.

You have done your research before this meeting so you also know the "all-in" cost at any college you are talking with so you can compare "apples to apples". A 25% scholarship to a private school is not the same as a 25% scholarship to a state school; your share of the actual cost can be dramatically different. Financially you might be better off with a 25% scholarship at one school than a 50% scholarship at another.

Both the Coach and the Admissions officers are going to ask you what you are "looking for" in a college or university. What you're looking for can range from your expectations regarding playing time to whether or not the school has a good track record placing their graduates in the major you want to study. Decide early what is important to you. Is it location? School size? Playing time? Tradition? Graduate placement? Once again, be honest with this answer. That is the best way for a recruit and a coach to determine whether or not the school is a good fit. This is not a time to tell them what you think they want to hear. This is your future.

Attend Camps/Combines/Showcases that make sense

Do your research. Just as anybody can declare they are a "recruiter" and start working as one, anyone can put together a Camp, Combine or Showcase.

In most cases a Combine's purpose is to provide official numbers; those numbers are only important if a college will accept them. If a

Combine has a long list of athletes who ran a 4.3, benched 35 Reps and jumped 44" in the Vertical Test, pass on that combine; college coaches will. Combines who post results online on their websites, are long established like the NUC Combines in Football, or Perfect Game for Baseball, or those run by Coaches who work with Elite athletes are probably the best place to start looking.

For Showcases, it's all about who is going to be there, how well the Showcase documents your performance and what the follow up is.

Camps are different than Combines and Showcases. You have to decide if your goal in going to a camp is to learn more in your sport or to be seen. As you research camps keep the goal in mind. There are amazing camps whose purpose is to teach and there are excellent camps who have days when college coaches come to watch.

Follow Up Emails
Send follow up emails to the colleges that you haven't heard back from. You are not being a pest; you are just following up. Add in new information or include your SAT/ACT scores. Note in your spreadsheet or on your digital file that you have contacted the coach, the date of contact and whom you have copied on the email.

Keep in contact with coaches who have contacted you

While it sounds obvious, you'd be surprised at how many student-athletes fill out a recruiting form or respond to an email and then assume that they're finished. If you are interested in a program you should continue the conversation. Ask questions via email; ask if the coach needs any additional information. Retweet and share the programs' information on social media. You can safely email a coach every 2 weeks. Your interest has to be active; passive athletes don't win games or get recruited.

Financial Aid Forms

Always assume that you are not going to get an Athletic Scholarship. If you do, great. But if you don't then you have to be prepared. Get your financial aid forms in order and in as soon as possible.

Have your Guidance Counselor work with you on the timetables for financial aid. States have different deadlines and they differ from the Federal Deadlines. Individual colleges also have deadlines.

You can find Federal Student Aid Deadlines and applications at:
https://fafsa.ed.gov/deadlines.html
Fill out your FAFSA. (Free Application for Federal Student Aid) This is a form required by the government in order to apply for any federal

education aid program. The FAFSA is used to determine the expected family contribution (EFC) based on family financial information. A FAFSA is used to determine the specific Federal Student Aid programs that can contribute to a student's total financial package and in what proportions. Go to www.fafsa.ed.gov for more information.

Now this is important; if you get an offer don't stop the process.

I know that once an offer comes in from a school, it is really tempting to think you are finished. Offers from college coaches are made in good faith but any number of factors can derail the process. Until you sign a NLI or have a written offer that is binding, you want to continue your recruiting efforts.

Don't compare
Don't compare your recruiting journey to your friends/teammates. It can be really disconcerting to open your social media and see an announcement from a friend of an offer especially if you haven't gotten much interest yet. Of course you're happy for them, but you're also concerned for yourself. As an athlete you know that once you start thinking you're defeated you're much closer to losing.

Every College Coach runs his or her program differently and each year there are differences in their recruiting timing. Each sport has a different timetable. Stick to your own gameplan.

SAT/ACT Scores
Evaluate your SAT/ACT scores and decide if you are going to take either of the tests again.

If you are going to take the test again, put together a study plan and mark the dates to register in your calendar.

Work on the areas of the tests that gave you the most difficulty, that's the only way you're going to improve.

Don't get discouraged
Only 2% of high school athletes are "highly recruited." It is not uncommon for an athlete with exceptional skills and stats to go unnoticed, especially by NCAA Division II, Division III or NAIA schools that have limited recruiting budgets. If you're not hearing from coaches, you may have to put in more work. Remember that, to some extent, your recruiting process is a numbers game. Reach out to more colleges. The more appropriate colleges you reach out to, the better your chance of finding a roster sport and/or scholarship.
You have to apply the same mental toughness standards to recruiting that you apply to sports. Getting discouraged drains your energy just at the point when you need it!

Senior Year   Senior Checklist

	Take Serious Senior Courses
	Review and update your Favorites List
	Retake the SAT/ACT if necessary
	Meet with your Coach
	Go on Official Visits
	Dial down on reaching out to colleges
	Submit all Financial Aid Forms
	Actions to take after you have a spot
	Have Final Transcripts sent to NCAA/NAIA

Go on Official visits
An Official visit will be offered to you if you are of very real interest to a coach and that school has official visits. NCAA College coaches can only offer a specific number of Official visits and you can only go on five, so be sure that the college/university is one you legitimately would like to attend so you are not wasting your time and their time. Official visits give you a chance to meet the people you'll be playing with and to absorb the team and school culture. But, they are also an extended interview. Your behavior during the visit will be a factor in the College Coach's final decision.

Many sports at many schools don't have the budget for "official" visits, so don't immediately assume you're doomed if you are not invited on one.

Take serious Senior courses
Do not take fluff courses your Senior year. The quality of your Senior courses is obvious when coaches and colleges look at your course load and it does not leave a favorable impression if you're taking it easy. More importantly, easy courses do nothing to prepare you for the time and energy demands of being a college athlete.

Grades from your previous Core courses are now locked for NCAA eligibility; however, you still need to maintain the required minimum Core

Course GPA. Senior grades are also important for your NAIA GPA requirements.

Retake the SAT/ACT if you think that you can get a higher score

Ask that those scores be sent to the NCAA and/or NAIA Eligibility centers when you register for the test. Use the SAT Score Choice for this test; you can check that you did get better scores before they are sent out.

The reality check for retaking the SAT/ACT is whether you have worked to do better on the test. Just because you're a year older doesn't mean your scores are going to increase.

Dial down on reaching out to colleges
If you haven't found your college, don't panic but you do want to step up your efforts. You may have to add to the schools that you have contacted and reach out to more coaches. You may have to expand the geographic area that you are searching in. Look at the least important variables in your former decisions of what college to reach out to and see if you can broaden those categories.

A note of caution: the beginning of Senior year is when unethical "recruiters" start bombarding student-athletes with promises that they can get you an athletic scholarship. They take advantage of that slight panic everyone feels when their future is not yet set. (Remember that Recruiters are recruiters simply because they say they are.) Reputable companies will never guarantee that they can get you an athletic scholarship or even a roster spot.

Review and update your Favorite Colleges List

At this point you have a better idea of both your skills level and your academic picture. You may find that schools you thought were "reach" schools have become viable options. You may find that some schools you thought suited you really don't. Or a school may have recruited a class of Freshman who play your position and you have to decide if you want to sit the bench for your first years. Keep in mind that most students do not know what colleges they've been accepted into until the spring of Senior year. There is time as long as you are working towards your goal.

Meet with your coach to review his or her assessment of your abilities

This year's meeting is going to be different than the meetings in previous years; you are now at the level Coaches look to for their leaders, whether that be quiet leaders who keep people level, organizational leaders or loud advocates of the program. That is going to figure into the assessment.

Have a list of questions that you want to ask your coach, both about colleges and about your skills and play. You also want to talk to other coaches who have worked with you on conditioning, skills or other teams. Each person can add valuable information if you listen objectively.

Keep in contact with College Coaches
Keep in steady contact with Coaches who have contacted you from schools you have interest in. Tag or DM Coaches with news you share about your sports career, your extracurricular activities and your team. Email any questions to the coach or call if that is the method of communication you worked out with them.

Social Media is not, however, the place to announce your commitment to a school until you have personally let other coaches whom you been dealing with know your decision. The other coaches have put time and invested effort into your recruiting journey; it is expected you will pick up the phone and let them know that you will be going to another school as soon as that is firm. College Coaching is a small world, a reputation for being unethical or rude will haunt you long after the recruiting is done.

Finalize Finances
Work on squaring away your financial aid needs. There are numerous scholarship opportunities

out there. Free sites like
http://www.studentscholarshipsearch.com can
be a good resource for scholarships and
grants.   The College Board has a scholarship
finder function on their website also. Keep in
mind that most scholarships and grants can be
combined with others scholarships and grants,
work options and athletic scholarships.

After You Sign
Once you have accepted a roster spot or
scholarship from a school be certain you
understand your obligations so you keep that
offer. The signing of a National Letter of Intent
or an agreement is a tremendous
accomplishment but not the end of your journey.

The recruiting process is over, but your
collegiate career is just beginning. It's not time
to hit the brakes; it's time to accelerate. You
don't just want to show up to college; you want
to be ready to go from day one.

Most athletes want to play at college and not just
sit on the bench. In order for that to happen, you
have to be ready once you step foot on campus.
College coaches want you to show up strong
and well-conditioned. You should arrive in the
best condition of your life; that reaffirms to the
coaches that they made a good decision on you
and helps build respect and trust. You have one
shot at being a college athlete, there is no
excuse to not be 100% physically prepared.

Many scholarship athletes come to college expecting to have significant playing time immediately, but the truth is, there are no guarantees. You are not the only player the coaches have signed. In addition to competing for playing time with the new crop of signees, you will also be competing for playing time against current players on the roster, the proven veterans. That gives them an advantage. You need to be ready to compete at the first practice.

After you sign, if you really want to play as quickly as possible, then it's not a bad idea to "size up" the roster:

> •Determine who you will be competing against for playing time. If they are upperclassmen with game experience, do your best job to find out the secret to their success within the program. There is a reason they play, so figure out what they do well and commit to doing it better.

> •How many players are there at your position and how do you stack up against those players? You might want to spend additional time in the weight room or refining your skills before you hit campus.

> •Talk to the coaches and ask them what you need to do to contribute to

the team. Be specific and ask for specific answers.

•Let's face it, playing a sport in college is not like a full time job, it is a full time job. Scholarship athletes can spend as much as 50-60 hours per week at practice, watching game film, lifting weights and preparing for games. Being a college athlete is a huge commitment; be mentally prepared for the grind.

•College life is an adjustment for all students. You will be on your own for the first time, you need to learn how to manage your time and if you add the requirements of being part of a team, it can be overwhelming. The athletes who take the time to plan their class schedule generally adjust much faster and play sooner.

Important: At the end of Senior Year have your final transcripts sent to the NCAA and/or NAIA. Transcripts must come from your school.

Post Season

Why it's Worth It

First, this is all worth it because you get to play a sport you love for another few years at a competitive level.

When I asked a former college athlete "what was the best part of playing college sports?" His answer was: "Everything is the best part, it's AWESOME…the players, coaches and trainers all working together every day for one goal, pushing each other and working through good times and bad times. We will be friends for life." In one sentence he covered everything about playing college sports. Learning teamwork, discipline, confidence, hard work, mental toughness, leadership and lasting relationships that are established are lifelong skills. The intangible advantages of playing college sports may well outweigh the obvious benefit of a college scholarship. Let's face it; a very small percentage of college athletes go on to play professionally. Given that, it's important to know the role college athletes can play in the "real world."

Future Employers Look for Intangibles

"Everybody thinks sports is about winning. For me, it's more about losing and then figuring out a way to win. It's those things that make working with athletes and hiring former athletes a reasonable thing to consider." Dick Cashin One Equity Partners.

Look at a CEO's background and you'll probably find they were a high school and/or a college athlete.

EBay CEO Meg Whitman was on the lacrosse and squash teams at Princeton. Lynn Laverty Elsenhans was a member of the first Rice Women's Basketball team and subsequently became the first women to run a major oil company; she's the Sunoco CEO. Mondelēz International CEO Irene Rosenfeld played Basketball at Cornell. IBM CEO Samuel Palmisano was a star offensive center on the Johns Hopkins football team and was offered a tryout with the NFL's Oakland Raiders. Before running the Whole Foods team, CEO Walter Robb played midfield and center back on the Stanford soccer team. Jeffrey Immelt, General Electric's CEO was an offensive tackle at Dartmouth:

"Not every play works, not every situation works, but you've got to figure it out, and there's always a next play. And I think all of those things just happen to stick with you for a lot of your life, and in my case for my whole life. This essence of trying to build a culture of excellence that I learned in sports I very much brought to the business world."

Prospective employers are looking for employees who go the extra mile. Balancing the hours of practice and games while going to college is difficult, and it is an indication of a student's work ethic. While it might be hard to argue that sports have a direct correlation to higher incomes, promotions, and better jobs, there is no question that the leadership skills, development of teamwork, time management, and determination of many athletes surely help prepare athletes for the working world.

"If you try out for a basketball team but quit in the middle of the first game, or if you choose not to pass the ball to your talented teammate because you don't like her, or if you are unwilling to spend extra hours to work on a weakness, you aren't going to get very far. Athletics teach fundamentals for success and that is why both men and women executives like to hire athletes." Donna de Varona, Olympic Champion and adviser to EY's Women Athletes Business Network

Athletes are goal-oriented, something employers look for in employees. Most college athletes started playing their sport at the age of four or five. They have been competing their entire life. They know how to set goals and they work hard to achieve them. Most athletes talented enough to play in college have set goals every year, every season and every game.

College athletes also generally know how to ignore distractions and focus on the task at hand. In the digitally connected world that skill stands out. Today's companies are facing an uphill battle against digital distractions cutting into productive time. Athletes know how to blank out distractions, put up that mental wall and get things done.

Zig Ziglar once said, "There is no elevator to success, you have to take the stairs." Every college athlete learns this lesson, the hard way. College athletes are hard workers and become good time managers. Playing college sports is like having a job while you are going to school. It is a commitment. Student-athletes have multiple responsibilities including attending class, homework, strength training, conditioning, practice, travel and games. In addition, they have to find the time to eat and occasionally catch Sports Center. Any student that can pull all that off and maintain a good GPA is an excellent candidate for employment.

Add into the mix that college athletes are good teammates and good teammates make good employees. The ability to work with others toward a common goal as a team is a great attribute for an employee. Part of being a good teammate includes being coachable, respectful and having the attitude that the goals of the team are more important than the goals of the individual. Most college coaches will drive this point home with all their athletes and future employees eventually benefit from that training.

Many businesses are focused on providing a team environment in the workplace, as evidenced by the discussion of the importance of teamwork in numerous publications like the Harvard Business Review. In fact, some companies have said that they look specifically to hire former athletes, because of their ability to work as a team. By the time they graduate from college, most have been a member of a team for 16 to 18 years and being a good teammate has become a habit. The majority of former student-athletes say that being part of a team while participating in college sports prepared them for life after graduation.

Then, college athletes tend to be leaders. In today's society athletes are looked at as leaders and learn early on how to deal with the pressure and promise of that. 14 of the last 19 United States Presidents participated in college athletics. To be a good leader you have to be confident, resilient, a strong communicator and willing to put the team's goals ahead of your own. Employers want to hire employees that have the potential to become leaders in their company.

There is no better place to learn the skills of selflessness and leadership than on the playing field or court.

The Life Lessons learned in sports serve you well

What are the life lessons learned by most college athletes? The list is long, but it certainly includes teamwork, work ethic, and time management. Most college athletes are put into a situation where they have to learn these traits or they just don't survive. Let's be honest; playing college sports is a commitment. You have to be disciplined and work hard or you won't make the grades necessary to stay eligible. Winning with respect, losing with dignity and learning from both are lessons that last a lifetime.

Relationships

At the top of the list of benefits from playing college sports are the relationships established while being a part of a team. I had a conversation last year with a medical supplies salesman from Tucson, Arizona who played Division III football 23 years ago. He has a son and a daughter who both wanted to play their sport in college. He is really working hard to help them realize their dream. Why? Because he says playing college football was one of the best experiences in his life.

Here is the story he told me…. Several years ago his college roommate (and teammate) was diagnosed with Lou Gehrig's disease. He decided to host a dinner of former teammates to "love on his roommate." He sent invitations and hoped at least a few of the guys could come. Fifty-three teammates showed up for the dinner, with most of them flying in from their homes scattered all over the country. It was one of the most moving events in his life. They weren't all "best friends," but they had a "connection."

If you are lucky enough to have the talent to play intercollegiate sports, don't miss out on the opportunity. Take control of the process and shape your future.

Appendix 1: Recruiting Rules and Definitions

Athletes love acronyms right? Half of us don't even think that there's a bunch of words behind the NFL, NHL, WNT, MLB, or NBA; the acronyms have become the way we think of that entity. College recruiting loves acronyms too. You're going to be dealing with a group of them over the next few years; memorize them early, it saves a lot of brain power.

NCAA, NAIA and NJCAA
The largest organization governing sports in colleges and universities in the USA is the NCAA, the National Collegiate Athletic Association; it has about 1200 member institutions. The NCAA is divided into three divisions, DI, DII, DIII and each division has different rules. To complicate it a little more, each sport also has its own rules within its Division. Download the *NCAA Guide for the College Bound Student Athlete* and keep it handy.
http://www.ncaapublications.com/DownloadPublication.aspx?download=CBSA16.pdf

NCAA DI schools usually have the largest student population and manage the largest budget. http://www.ncaa.org/DI For DI Football (and only football) the Division is further broken up by Football Bowl Subdivision (they participate in Bowl Games,) Football Championship

Subdivision (they participate in an NCAA run Football Championship) and then those schools that don't sponsor a Football Championship event. DI schools offer athletic scholarships although, contrary to popular belief, most athletic scholarships are partial scholarships.

Contrary to popular belief, DI schools do not often offer full ride scholarships for most sports. Full ride scholarships are offered in "head count" sports but not equivalency sports.

A head count sport means that there is a set number of scholarships that can be given out for a team and that scholarship money can't be divided differently. So, if there are 85 scholarships allowed in a DI Football program, there are 85 athletes with scholarships; the school can't divide scholarship money among more athletes.

Head Count Scholarship Sports:
Football (DI FBS only)

Basketball (DI men's and women's)

Tennis (DI women only)

Gymnastics (DI women only)

Volleyball (DI women only)

Equivalency Scholarship Sports:

All other DI sports are equivalency sports. Equivalency sports have limits on the number of scholarships but not on how that scholarship money is divided up. Basically, if a team has 10 scholarships, the total dollar amount of those 10 scholarships can be divided among the athletes on the team in partial scholarships at the coach's discretion.

All DII sports are equivalency sports.

If you are watching a college game on television you are probably watching a DI program play.

DII   There are approximately 300 NCAA colleges and universities that are DII schools. DII schools usually have a smaller student population and place an emphasis on a balance between athletics and academics. They'll tend to have smaller athletic budgets and offer a "partial-scholarship" model for financial aid, so most financial aid is a mixture of athletic scholarships, grants, academic aid and employment. DII schools' Championships are decided at National Championship Festivals; the festivals are a number of national championships held at the same site over several days.
http://www.ncaa.org/DII

To play at NCAA DI and DII schools you have to register and qualify; you start the registration process at the NCAA Eligibility Center website. (Don't jump there now, we'll go through registration a little later on.)

DIII is the largest division in the NCAA; DIII schools make up about 40% of NCAA membership. DIII schools offer financial aid in various forms but don't offer athletic scholarships. Although DIII schools provide rigorous athletics, their emphasis is on the student-athlete college experience. Athletics may give you a slight admissions edge in an equal competition with another candidate but at a DIII school your grades and overall resume are really the primary qualification.
http://www.ncaa.org/DIII

Summary: The NCAA has DI, DII, DIII schools. Each Division has its own set of rules. Each sport within each division also has its own timetable and rules. Do not get overwhelmed, you only have to worry about your particular sport.

NAIA

The National Association of Intercollegiate Athletics or NAIA oversees programs that are usually smaller than those in the NCAA; NAIA governs 15 Men's Sports and 15 Women's Sports at their member schools. Each of those sports has a Championship competition.

The NAIA also has an Eligibility Center and student-athletes have to qualify to be able to play sports at an NAIA school; their academic standards allow you to qualify on 2 out of 3 criteria. Although not as well-known as the

NCAA, NAIA schools invest $500,000,000 in scholarships in more than 65,000 student-athletes each year.

This is an association that is totally separate from the NCAA so even if you have registered with the NCAA you still have to register with the NAIA to play at an NAIA school.http://www.playnaia.org
NAIA Guide for the College Bound Athlete
http://www.playnaia.org/d/NAIA_GuidefortheColl egeBoundStudent.pdf

Summary: The NAIA programs also offer athletic scholarships, most of those are partial scholarships. NAIA academic requirements for eligibility are slightly lower than the NCAA although you still have to academically qualify for each individual school.

Eligibility Fees

Both the NCAA and NAIA charge a fee when you sign up in their Eligibility Center. (NCAA is $75 and NAIA $70 for US and Canadian Students in 2015) If you are eligible for a fee waiver from the College Board (SAT) or the (ACT) then the NCAA and NAIA will waive the eligibility fee. The NAIA also waives the eligibility fee if you qualify for a free or reduced price lunch at your school or get a Pell grant of $4500.00 or more.

And, I hate to tell you but both NCAA and NAIA schools currently require either SAT or ACT scores and those scores count towards eligibility.

As you plan to play in your future remember, scholarships and financial aid are given by individual colleges and universities, not by the NCAA or NAIA. They just make sure you are eligible to play according to their criteria.

Don't fall asleep yet, just one more category to go.

Junior Colleges/Community Colleges. Junior colleges are viable options for some athletes and several have strong athletic programs. Ready for the next acronyms? 525 JUCOs (Junior Colleges) are governed by the National Junior College Athletic Association (NJCAA) which also divides schools into DI, DII and DIII.

The NJCAA functions differently than the NCAA and NAIA; it awards both partial and full scholarships to athletes directly. In order to play at a NJCAA school you have to be a full time student of the school.

Summary: JUCOs are governed by the NJCAA and the NJCAA awards the athletic scholarships to JUCO athletes.

NCAA Vocabulary

Think you would like to play at an NCAA school? There are a slew of terms used in the NCAA recruiting process and you should understand what they mean or half of what you read will be a total mystery. Most of the terms revolve around when coaches can talk to prospective athletes and the NCAA is strict about these rules. Here's what you need to add to your vocabulary:

Contact

An exchange of information between a coaching staff and a prospective student-athlete. Contacts include camp brochures, letters, questionnaires, emails, phone call and tape requests.

Contact Period: All in

During this time the coach can talk to you face-to-face on or off campus, watch your competitions, visit your high school, email, phone, etc. Any communications are allowed to be initiated by the coach, although they can only contact you in person once a week during this time.

Evaluation Period: Watch and Virtual

The coach can watch you compete and visit your High School, email, phone etc. But, they can't talk to you face-to-face off of their campus. They can talk to you face-to-face on their campus.

Dead Period: Virtual Only
A coach can't have any in person contact with the player or the player's family. The coach can, however call, write, email, DM. Think of it as an "electronic only" time.

Quiet period: On Campus and Virtual
The coach can't have in person contact with you off the college campus but you can visit the campus. The coach can't watch you compete unless you are on their campus competing. The coach can write, email, call or DM.

Recruiting Calendars:
Each NCAA sport has their own recruiting calendar that spells out the Contact, Evaluations, Quiet and Dead Periods each year. Those periods depend on the time of year the sport is usually played in high school; sports differ significantly. However, the dates of each sport's contact, evaluation, quiet and dead periods generally don't change that much from year to year so you can use the current year's calendar as a general guideline in your planning.

Focus on your sport, don't panic when someone from another sport talks about coaches calling or emailing them, each sport has a different recruiting rhythm.

You need to know when the coaches from your sport can contact you and in what way they can contact you throughout the calendar year. So highlight your mobile calendar using a different color for each of the periods. (Don't use black for the dead period - it's a pain to change all the fonts to white. Try grey.)

Coaches can normally respond at any time digitally if you initiate the contact. So if you DM a coach your Freshman year about their program, they can respond on DM.

A Note to Parents: The same restrictions apply to parents as to the student-athlete. Don't try to circumvent the rules, it will hurt your child.

Official and Unofficial Visits
The big difference between an Official and Unofficial visit is that an Official Visit is paid for by the college/university. An Unofficial visit is paid for by the student-athlete or their guardian(s).   During an Unofficial visit you can only accept 3 tickets to a home sporting event from the school, anything else is a violation of recruiting rules.

The first dates you are eligible for an official visit differs for each sport. For Men's Basketball you can take an official visit starting January 1 of your Junior Year while most sport's first official visit can't occur until the first day of classes your Senior year. Those are spelled out on the NCAA website for each sport.

Keep all these "differs for each sport" in mind. If you play Lacrosse and your best friend plays Basketball you are not on the same timeline for recruiting. Don't get caught in the "but he/she heard from Colleges and I haven't" spiral.

National Letter of Intent (NCAA)
You already know that student-athletes sign National Letters of Intent because the signings are, justifiably, accompanied by a lot of ceremony and covered by the press. A National Letter of Intent is a contract between you and an NCAA school. The school promises to provide a specified amount of financial aid as long as you remain eligible and the student-athlete agrees to go to that school and play for that program. If you break the NLI you cannot play at any NCAA institution for a year.

Don't confuse the NLI with a "commitment" to a school. A commitment means that you and the school have a verbal, non-binding agreement. Either the player or the school's coaching staff can change their mind about a commitment.

Here's the language for this part of the recruiting journey.

Recruit
Just because someone calls you a recruit doesn't mean that they are offering to have you play at their school or going to offer you a scholarship. Recruit is a general term that's often applied to every competitor who might play at the school or who has an interest in playing at the school.

Recruiting List
Athletes the coaches at an institution are actively recruiting. Typically, a student-athlete is not added to this list until the athlete has been evaluated.

Commitment
When you commit to a school you have received a verbal offer from the legitimate coaching staff to play for the school and have agreed to go to the school and play there. It is not a binding agreement. A lot of things can happen between a verbal agreement and a firm "agreement" or National Letter of Intent if you're DI, DII NCAA. If the coaching staff changes, if the team loses specific players to injuries or transfers, if a spectacular player decides to commit to the school, the offer may not hold. Student-athletes have also been known to change their minds after they have committed to a specific program.

Commitments are usually made in good faith by both the athlete and the College Coaching staff; they can change so plan accordingly.

Over the last few years we have also seen offers being made to student-athletes from catfished accounts. If you get an offer via Direct Messaging, confirm it with the coaching staff at their email addresses.

Verbal Commitment
A student verbally indicates that he/she plans to attend a college or university to play college sports. A verbal commitment is not binding, although it is a generally accepted method of commitment.

Application Waiver
A college coach waives the fee for applying to the college or university so that you can apply without paying the fee. Generally, the fee then comes out of the Athletic budget.

Early Decision
An athletic early decision differs from the general college early decision. Early decision in recruiting is a binding agreement where the student-athlete accepts an offer before signing day.

Gray Shirt
A Student who is recruited out of high school, but delays full-time enrollment.

Red Shirt
A student who does not compete in any competition during a full academic year.

Walk-on
A student who does not receive an athletic scholarship but who is a member of the team.

Academic Rules

Before you can play for a college or university you have to be accepted into the school. That means you have to qualify for the school academically. Despite the wild rumors you hear about a player who was failing every class and bombed the SATs playing at Harvard; it doesn't happen in real life. Athletics may give you an edge if you and another candidate are equally qualified. If you are one of the best players in the nation, the Athletic Department might go to bat for you with Admissions as long as you are academically eligible by NCAA or NAIA standards. But for most student-athletes their grades and test scores are extremely important.

NCAA DI

There is a sliding scale which adds your SAT/ACT scores to your core course GPA (Grade Point Average), the combination determines your eligibility. First, you must have a minimum 2.3 core course GPA on a scale of 4.0 to be eligible. No College program can get around that. The NCAA requires specific courses and those are the core courses. The lower your core course GPA, the higher your SAT/ACT score has to be. For a 2.3 core course GPA you a minimum 900 on your Verbal and Math SAT or combined 75 on your ACT. For a 3.0 core course GPA you need a score of 620 on your SAT Verbal and Math or a combined 52 on the

ACT.   As your core course GPA rises the required test scores fall. (The combined ACT score is a sum of the following four sections: English, mathematics, reading and science.)

Now, and this is important, the core course GPA is not the same as the GPA your school shows. The NCAA only calculates your GPA based on eligible core courses.

For the 2016 graduating class there are 16 core courses for NCAA DI:

4 years of English
3 years of math (Algebra I or higher)
2 years of natural/physical science (1 year of lab if offered)
1 year of additional English, math or natural/physical science
2 years of social science
4 years of additional courses (any area above, foreign language or comparative religion/philosophy)

You can check if the courses you are planning on taking (or are taking) qualify using the NCAA tool which tells you which courses in your particular school are accepted.
https://web3.ncaa.org/hsportal/exec/hsAction?hsActionSubmit=searchHighSchool

The second academic requirement is that courses are locked; and this is really important. Before the beginning of your 7th semester (end of Junior year for most of you), the grades in your core courses are locked. You can't re-take a course during your Senior year and substitute the grade in the core course GPA. That's a change for everyone who graduates after 2015.

NCAA DII

NCAA DII requires 16 core courses. 10 of these have to be completed before your Senior year. (7th semester) 7 of those 10 courses have to be in English, math or natural/physical science.

NCAA DII Eligibility requires a minimum SAT score of 820 or an ACT sum score of 68 and a minimum 2.0 GPA in core courses.

We're only talking about your athletic eligibility here; you have to meet the eligibility standards of the college or university also.

NCAA DIII

DIII academic eligibility is based on the requirements of each individual school and those requirements vary widely. University of Wisconsin-Oshkos, for example, requires Algebra, Algebra II and Geometry not just 3 math courses and their average GPA of accepted students was 3.37 in 2015. Wheaton

College in Massachusetts is an SAT/ACT optional school, possibly because 40% of their freshman are in the top 10% of their graduating class. Tufts in nearby Boston requires SATs or ACTs with the range of their SAT Math 690-770. Colorado College, in Colorado Springs CO, requires standardized testing but may waive that requirement. You get the idea, the requirements for admission vary widely and you need to know your freshman year what those requirements are in order to plan your high school courses correctly.

NAIA

The NAIA determines eligibility at the end of your Senior year unless you have a 3.0 overall GPA at the end of your Junior year. If you do, you can qualify for early decision eligibility. You can also get early decision after the first semester of your senior year if you have a 2.5 overall GPA and the minimum requirements on your SAT or ACT. (You are required to have a minimum 18 on the ACT or 860 on the SAT) A major difference between NCAA and NAIA academic eligibility is that the NAIA uses your general GPA (all your courses) instead of a core GPA.

☐

Appendix 2: The Difference Between Being Noticed and Being Recruited

Every student-athlete starts in the same place, just trying to get noticed. Once you are noticed, the goal is to be recruited. It is really important to understand where you are, so you can identify what needs to be done. Many prospects and their parents think they are being recruited when they are not.

You are not being recruited if:

You are not being recruited if you receive information from college admission offices. Well, you are actually being recruited to become a student at those schools, but not a student-athlete. These letters have nothing to do with being recruited to be an athlete in college. These letters are a part of a direct-mail campaign and although those schools might like you to become a student, that is all it means.

You are not being recruited if you get invited to a camp. There may be legitimate recruits at the camps, but 99% of the attendees are not on the school's "short list" of scholarship candidates.

You are not being recruited if a college coach "views" your profile on a recruiting website. While a quality profile with verified statistics and video can be helpful, coaches are usually checking information on someone they might be interested in.

You are not being recruited if a college coach sees you play at a game or tournament. College coaches show up at tournaments and games to watch specific athletes. Sure, it might help if you return a kick for a touchdown or score three goals, but unfortunately it may not help a lot.

You've been noticed, but you are not being recruited

You've been noticed if you receive a letter or email from a college coach asking you to fill out a recruiting questionnaire. Being recognized or noticed is the initial stage in earning a roster spot or scholarship. Make sure you complete the questionnaire right away and fill it out as accurately as possible. The questionnaire will help the coach determine if you are a good candidate for his or her program and may be a start to being recruited.

You've been noticed if your current coach gets an inquiry about you from a college coach. This is a clear indication that the school at least has interest in you as a player. Remember, your current coach is the most credible source to vouch for your abilities and character. Your coach's response can go a long way toward you actually being recruited.

You've been noticed if you receive a letter or email that a coach plans to "keep up with you". They may also ask for a highlight video or game film. If this happens, you are getting closer to being a legitimate recruit, but you're not there yet.

You've been noticed if you receive a personal response to an email or message you sent to a coach. Apparently, something in your email piqued their interest, now it's time to close the deal. Have your current coach contact the college coach on your behalf within a reasonable period of time. Don't wait several weeks before you take action.

You are being recruited

You are being recruited if college coaches are calling you at home, or are communicating with you on a regular basis. A telephone call from a college coach is a great indication that there is real interest in you as an athlete. Relax and be yourself. Let the coach get to know your personality.

You are being recruited if a college coach comes to one of your games to specifically see you play. College coaches are extremely busy, so if they take the time to attend one of your games, they are interested. Understand that they realize you aren't going to score 30 points every game or go 4 for 4 at the plate. They can tell everything they need to know by just watching you play. If you do turn the ball over or commit an error, your reaction to the mistake is more important than the mistake itself.

You are being recruited if you are asked to go on an official visit. Official visits are not given to every recruit. An official visit is any visit to a college campus by a college-bound student-athlete or his or her parents, paid for by the college. If you are invited on an official visit, make the most of it. Remember, you can only have one official visit per school and five official visits total.

Appendix 3: Scholarships, Teams, Athletes

The maximum # of scholarships that are offered per sport by any 1 college or university.

Sport	NCAA DI FBS	NCAA DI FCS	NCAA DII	NAIA	NJCAA
Baseball	11.7	N/A	9	12	24
Women's Basketball	15	N/A	10	11	15
Men's Basketball	13	N/A	10	11	15
Women's Cross Country	18	N/A	12.6	5	10
Men's Cross Country	12.6*	N/A	12.6*	5	10
Football	85	63	36	24	85
Women's Golf	6	N/A	5.4	5	8
Men's Golf	4.5	N/A	3.6	5	8
Women's Ice Hockey	18	N/A	18	0	0
Men's Ice Hockey	18	N/A	13.5	0	16
Field Hockey	12	N/A	6.3	0	0
Women's Lacrosse	12	N/A	9.9	0	20
Men's Lacrosse	12.6	N/A	10.8	0	20

Women's Soccer	12	N/A	9.9	12	18
Men's Soccer	9.9	N/A	9	12	18
Softball	12	N/A	7.2	10	24
Women's Swimming & Diving	9.9	N/A	9	8	15
Men's Swimming & Diving	8.1	N/A	0	8	15
Women's Tennis	8	N/A	6	5	0
Men's Tennis	4.5	N/A	4.5	5	0
Women's Track & Field	18	N/A	12.7	12	20
Men's Track & Field	12.6	N/A	12.7	12	20
Women's Volleyball	12	N/A	6	5	14
Men's Volleyball	4.5	N/A	4.5	0	0
Women's Water Polo	8	N/A	8	0	0
Men's Water Polo	4.5	N/A	4.5	0	0
Wrestling	9.9	N/A	9	2	16

* Track and Cross Country share scholarship money so the total $s are divided between the two sports.

Total teams in US Colleges and Universities (2014)

Sport	NCAA DI FBS	NCAA DI FCS	NCAA DII	NCAA DIII	NAIA	NJCAA
Baseball	294	N/A	262	360	208	393
Women's Basketball	349	N/A	307	442	229	406
Men's Basketball	351	N/A	309	447	236	441
Women's Cross Country	347	N/A	289	422	201	135
Men's Cross Country	318	N/A	260	401	195	125
Football	128 (129)	125 (122)	170 (168)	246	84	140
Women's Golf	263	N/A	181	184	146	54
Men's Golf	300	N/A	231	293	170	189
Women's Ice Hockey	29	N/A	9	52	1	1
Men's Ice Hockey	43	N/A	21	76	58	8
Field Hockey	79	N/A	29	162	1	-
Women's Lacrosse	103	N/A	85	257	16	15

Men's Lacrosse	66	N/A	57	218	18	30
Women's Soccer	310	N/A	225	426	223	201
Men's Soccer	198	N/A	179	400	217	229
Softball	286	N/A	264	392	205	369
Women's Swimming & Diving	197	N/A	89	251	23	14
Men's Swimming & Diving	135	N/A	66	218	20	13
Women's Tennis	323	N/A	230	375	107	78
Men's Tennis	265	N/A	170	331	96	69
Women's Track & Field	333	N/A	205	300	150	74
Men's Track & Field	282	N/A	184	288	146	68
Women's Volleyball	334	N/A	294	432	223	308
Men's Volleyball	23	N/A	17	69	22	--
Women's Water Polo	32	N/A	11	17	1	43
Men's Water Polo	22	N/A	7	15	2	--
Women's Wrestling	--	N/A	2	1	11	2
Men's Wrestling	73	N/A	60	93	43	40

SPORT	Approximate # Total Athletes
Baseball	55,410
Women's Basketball	27,710
Men's Basketball	32,190
Women's Cross Country	19,350
Men's Cross Country	18,220
Football	90,136
Women's Golf	6,638
Men's Golf	12,292
Women's Ice Hockey	2,150
Men's Ice Hockey	4,360
Field Hockey	5,885
Women's Lacrosse	10,870
Men's Lacrosse	13,857
Women's Soccer	37,760
Men's Soccer	37,890
Softball	30,874
Women's Swimming & Diving	13,679
Men's Swimming & Diving	10,893
Women's Tennis	10,869
Men's Tennis	10,060
Women's Track & Field	33,197
Men's Track & Field	33,955
Women's Volleyball	26,570
Men's Volleyball	2,314
Women's Water Polo	1,820
Men's Water Polo	1,670
Women's Wrestling	294
Men's Wrestling	9756

Appendix 4: Recruiting Videos

As I've said, different sports look for different things in highlight film, some sports /positions want to see a skill video and some also want to see a video of an entire game.

Highlight Video – 3 minutes maximum. This is exactly what it is labelled, a group of the highlights of your play. However, coaches also want to see how you interact on the field or court with your team and how you deal with pressure so this isn't 3 minutes of you shooting 3 pointers.

Your highlight video should have some of your personality in it. Coaches should have some sense of you after viewing it.

Do not add music, transitions, graphics, fast or slow motion; this is not going on Instagram.

Skills Video – Some sports and some specific positions want to see video of your skills.

Do not add commentary, music, fast/slow motion or replays; it's not an art project.

Before you begin putting your highlight video together, make an outline. Your best clip should go first, then list the skills/plays you want to highlight in the order of importance. It's easier to find pieces of video to put into your film when you know what you're looking for.

Put your name, school name, graduation year, and jersey number on the first frame of the video so the coaches know who to look for.

Put your name, address, phone number, email address, GPA and coach's name on the last frame of the video.

Your "get them interested" video should be 2-3 minutes. Depending on the sport you can also put together a 7-10 minute second video to send to coaches who have expressed interest in you; some sports, like basketball may ask to see an entire game on film if they have an interest in you.

Use Spot Shadows or arrows to highlight yourself. Don't ask a coach to pick you out of the pack.

Do not add music. Coaches want to see you, your play and your skills, your taste in music is irrelevant. (Actually many coaches watch the video with sound on mute.)

For game footage use the best footage you have against the best competition you play, whether that is in season, in summer or at a showcase or tournament.

Keep the video at the real pace, don't slow up a section or speed up a section.

Baseball

The video should be in segments: Hitting, Fielding, Running, and if it applies, Pitching. Do not add too many distractors, stats etc. other than the basic information.

For Hitting everyone should add in some actual game footage, coaches want to see the hit and then the run.

Pitchers: your video should have footage from behind the mound, open side view, and behind the plate. Coaches want to see mechanics, flight of the ball, movement, and velocity.
Middle infielders: your video should show defense, speed, and hitting

Corner Infielders: Routine outs, backhands, deep in the hole, charge plays, double plays, plays to the plate.

Outfielders: Coach Mazzoni of Sacred Heart University suggests "Have someone hit you legitimate fly balls, ground balls, and show the play from your prep step, read, catch, and throw. As an outfielder if your game is about speed, covering ground, that needs to come across in the video. If you are a bigger, strong armed, middle-of-the-order hitter type, then you likely want to put your hitting first in the video and feature your arm strength."

Catchers: blocking, throwing, receiving, as well as hitting skills. Coach Mazzoni's suggestion: "catch a pen with the camera closely on you. We want to see your hands and how you receive. Make part of the pen no one on and part of the time man on and when a ball is in the dirt, block and recover it. … As for pop times, this is really best shown in a game."

Additional References
http://www.collegecoachesbaseballcamp.com/2013/04/what-a-college-coach-wants-in-a-recruiting-video

The New England Catching Camp
http://www.catchingcamp.com/articles/important-content-for-recruiting-video-for-catchers
 has put together detailed specifics on what they have found to be most effective in a skills video. GetmyNameOut's website has detailed charts of both the skill and the camera angle for a baseball skills video.
http://www.getmynameout.com/content/equipment-room/tips-for-shooting-a-baseball-or-softball-skills-video

Basketball

First, make a general highlight tape, but then if a coach is interested in you ask what they want to see. Many Basketball coaches want to see an entire game film once they're interested in an athlete.   Some want 5 minutes of highlights and then 1 or 2 full game films. Interestingly Basketball coaches more than any other coaches say they want to see the flaws as well as the strengths in a total game situation.

For your highlight film, coaches want to see you play the game. For a point guard they need to see that you can control the tempo of the game, that you can defend and handle pressure as well as shoot.

Post Players: They're looking for speed, rebounding, shooting and the range of shooting, footwork, blocking, fundamentals, athleticism and "court vision."

Perimeter Players: Show Shooting range and ability, scoring, athleticism, "court vision" and ball handling.

Football

Do not add special effects, slow motion, replays or music. Arrows and spot shadows should only be used at the beginning of a play, do not keep them on you if they interfere with actually seeing the play. If you want to highlight yourself during the whole play only use spot shadows.

The film should have anywhere from 15 to 20 plays. Show the play through the whistle, coaches want to see how you handle the ball in total. Also, think about the skills required for the game and add some clips that show how you handle them. Add in Change of Direction running, some clips of work in the weight room; football fundamentals are important in the film.

Skills footage is only required for Kickers, Punters, and Long Snappers. For everyone else your highlight video should be clips from game film.

List Stats and Honors at the end of the video, not at the beginning.

Examples of good recruiting video:
http://bleacherreport.com/articles/1544333-college-football-recruiting-2014-the-10-most-impressive-recruit-videos/page/2

Lacrosse

Show Ability, Athleticism and Attitude.   Coaches are looking for fundamentals and athleticism; show that you're tough and a physical player. More than scoring goals or the defensive play the coaches look for what it takes to get to the goal or make the play. They're also want to see if you're a team player. Only goalies need a skills video along with a competition highlight video. In Lacrosse, plays that work in high school do not work against advanced opponents in college.

Watch college game film and see if you can match the skills in your own video to what you see in the college games.

Often if a coach is interested in you after viewing your highlight film you will be asked for a video of an entire game.

Soccer

Include passing, dribbling, finishing, volleying, heading and show co-ordination. The person recording your video should be as close as possible to the middle of the pitch and elevated with as much of an unrestricted view as possible. (No one wants to lose you and the ball because a column is in front of the camera.) The camera should be on a tripod so that the film is steady and doesn't bounce which makes it very difficult to concentrate on the film.

Goalkeepers should add skills footage to game highlights: Include diving both ways and high and low, punching crosses, sliding saves, goal kicks, punting.

For field players use 20 to 40 plays from your accumulated game footage. Center on ball handling, passing, goal kicks, steals and tackles and controlling the ball in runs.

Use a wide field view for most of the footage so that coaches can see your play within the context of the game and your team.

Softball

Hitting: The pitcher should throw batting practice type fastballs or you can use a pitching machine. With the camera angle the catcher area film 20-30 swings. Then film 15-20 swings with the camera 5 feet right of the plate for right handed hitters, 5 feet left of the plate for left handed hitters.

Base running: Swing, run to 1B. Swing run 1B 2B, Swing run bases to home.

Pitching: Approximately 20 varied pitches, 5 of them fastballs and 5 each of Rise, Drop, Curve.

InFielders: 8 Groundballs hit directly at you, 8 hit to your left, 8 hit to your right. 6-8 Slow Choppers hit at you. Fielding from SS position & throw to the 2B

Outfielders: Groundballs hit at you and throws to each base and home plate. Fly balls hit at you and throws to each base and home plate.

Volleyball

For Volleyball, college coaches will want to see a highlight film but also a skills film of your mechanics.

Highlight film for volleyball should be taken from behind the side of the court that you are playing on. That often requires special permission if someone other than a school sanctioned person is taking film, so take that into account. A Skills video can be shot from the side of the court and focus in on the individual player.

In a highlight film you want to show the player in the context of the game, how they are interacting with the entire team and the opposing team. For a skills video, you're showing your mastery of fundamentals.

Meet the Author

Fred Bastie

Fred Bastie was happily running Fred J. Bastie and Associates, a dynamic, growth-oriented certified public accounting firm with clients throughout the United States and Europe, when it was time for his children to start looking at colleges, and looking at colleges as athletes. His complete distaste for the sports recruiting help available led him to found Playced.com, a new concept in student-athlete college sports planning. Hundreds of interviews with college coaches and consultations with people like Gil Brandt led to develop a recruiting experience based on 21st century technology priced so that the majority of people can afford the help.

"I experienced the college recruiting process with both of my children. Like all parents, I wanted to help in any way I could. I spent hundreds of hours and a lot of money trying to find the right colleges. At times I was confused, frustrated and occasionally discouraged. Initially, I didn't believe that college coaches wanted to hear from prospective athletes. For that reason, I actually started the process with a few "big name" recruiting services, only to be turned off by their high pressure nature and sales tactics. Ultimately, the recruiting experience worked out for my kids! Unfortunately, I finally figured out the best way to approach college recruiting and didn't have any kids left!

The recruiting service industry has more than its fair share of companies taking advantage of well-meaning parents and confused student-athletes. It is not uncommon for a family to spend more money pursuing a college scholarship than the scholarship is worth. That just doesn't make sense! That is why I decided families needed a reasonably priced product (not a service) that could help high school athletes identify and pursue a college scholarship. I wanted it to be affordable for every athlete and use the traditional method of recruiting, preferred by college coaches."

Fred continues to run Fred J. Bastie and Associates but has added overseeing Playced.com to his work life. He also is a regular contributor to USA Today High School Sports as part of their recruiting partnership with Playced.

Playced.com is on the web at http://playced.com, Facebook at http://www.facebook.com/getplayced/ Twitter @Playced https://twitter.com/Playced Instagram @GetPlayced https://www.instagram.com/getplayced/

Illustrations Credits

Myth 1 Illustration, licensed to Playced.com
Myth 2 Illustration, Playced.com
Myth 3 Illustration, Playced.com
Myth 4 Illustration, Playced.com
Myth 5 Calendar licensed through Dreamtime
Myth 6 Illustration, Natasha Petrova licensed through Dreamtime
Myth 7 Illustration, licensed through Jantoon
Myth 8 Illustration, Rodney Gavely licensed through Dreamtime
Myth 9 Illustration, Alexey Bannykh licensed through Dreamtime
Myth 10 Photo, Elliott Burlingham licensed through Dreamtime
Develop a Recruiting Game Plan illustrations Playced.com

Recruiting Budget Photo licensed through Shutterstock
Parent Illustration 1 & 2 Ron Leishman licensed through clipartof
Parent illustration 3 AtStockIllustration licensed through clipartof
Parent Illustration 4 Playced.com

Interviews conducted by Ross Hawley / Fred Bastie:
Coach Brooks Thompson, Head Men's Basketball Coach The University of Texas at San Antonio
Theresa Romagnolo, Head Women's Soccer Coach Notre Dame University
Coach Russ Rose, Head Women's Volleyball Coach Penn State University
Jerry Ford, President Perfect Game
Erik Pulverenti, General Manager of Media for Hudl
Mack Brown, Former Head Football Coach at the University of Texas
Mike Candrea, Head Softball Coach at the University of Arizona

Made in the USA
Middletown, DE
06 July 2021

43742335R00106